play music better

Smart music practice tips

that work

Fiona Berry

Praise for Fiona Berry and
PLAY MUSIC BETTER

'Play music better' is essential reading for any musician wanting to develop their skill on their instrument. It takes a wonderful in-depth look at the most fundamental things involved in improving both technique and musicianship.

There are so many golden nuggets in this book, all of which, if followed, will lead the instrumentalist to a higher level skill set, and most importantly, make the age old dreaded practice session both fun and incredibly rewarding.

Practice is the cornerstone of potential excellence for any musician, and here, Fiona shows the reader how to do it the right way.

I recently decided to start practising after spending many years relying on what some may refer to as a 'natural gift'. Well unfortunately there's only so much you can do before you reach a dead end musically. The only way to excel and become a more accomplished player is, without doubt, to practice.

Her methods and informative layout cover everything from the approach to your practice session, relaxation, practicing the right things, the mental capacity we have to actually absorb things, and the correct amount of time to do all of the above.

All of her chapters are paramount in helping one become a better musician and I highly recommend the book to every musician out there, whether you're a beginner or more advanced player.

—**Max Beesley**- Distinguished and highly regarded musician, actor, producer, and writer.

With this book, Fiona Berry presents a surprisingly new and insightful look at how to obtain the most fun when playing music. Her observations and tips are to the point and they will make you obtain your musical goals faster and easier.

This book should be on your music stand right next to the piece of music you want to play or practise. Whenever you might feel less inspired, I urge you to read any chapter in this book and you will feel inspired again and ready to conquer and solve whatever musical problems you might have.

The mind can do wonderful tricks on you and Fiona Berry will unlock those musical problems and frustrations with logical, creative, and original advice. This book definitely brings the fun back in your music making!!!

—**Sebastiaan de Krom,** Renowned freelance drummer,
Principal Lecturer at Leeds Conservatoire,
Jazz drums teacher at Purcell School of Music, London,
Music Director of the National Jazz Youth Orchestra's Academy Big Band.

Fiona Berry has written an insightful, thoroughly practical, deeply personal and enormously helpful book.

The text is a common sense journey that is essential reading for teachers and learners alike. No stone is left unturned in the pursuit of healthy and enjoyable music making.

—**Jeffery Wilson,** Coordinator and Professor of Composition at Junior Guildhall School of Music, London, Professor of Saxophone at Royal Military School of Music, Director of Environ Music, Composer and Performer.

This book is an excellent guide to the often hidden mysteries of instrumental practice. Fiona Berry has produced a thoroughly comprehensive and insightful book.

The range of topics is broad, yet each is approached demonstrating a depth of research, and presented in a readable manner of great use to both student and teacher alike. A considerable achievement - highly recommended.

—**Richard Ingham FRSA,**
Honorary Professor of Jazz Education (ret'd), University of St Andrews, Visiting Tutor, University of Aberdeen
Director, XVI World Saxophone Congress
Editor, Cambridge Companion to the Saxophone (Cambridge University Press)
President, Clarinet and Saxophone Society of Great Britain

I worked with Fiona Berry for over 15 years and her pupils' results in Associated Board of the Royal Schools of Music and Trinity College London examinations were always remarkable. Not just the actual results themselves but the speed at which a child progressed from first lesson to attaining a distinction at Grade 8 was incredible.

She is truly one of the most inspiring teachers I have worked with and now, having read this book, I know why! If only my own teachers had taught me this way.

The insights and practical advice gleaned in this publication will be of huge benefit to all musicians, from beginners to advanced players alike. Keep it simple, get improvising and, most of all, Play Music Better ☺

—**Stephen Martin** BA (Hons), Director of Music (Bolton School 1998 – 2014)

Get Access to Training Videos, Resources and Free Audiobook!

READ THIS FIRST

Just to say thank you for buying my book, I would like to give you some extra video resources and my audiobook 100% FREE!

TO DOWNLOAD GO TO:

https://playmusicbetterbook.com/ resources or use the QR code with the camera app on your mobile phone.

Contents

Section 4

Perceive and Conquer

Section 5

Perform and Grow

Introduction

Are you one of those people who starts a new piece of music before you can play the one you're currently learning? While you'd love to play with fluency and ease, if truth be told, no piece you study ever achieves that level. Or perhaps you are the persistent sort who is happy to stay with a score for months and convince yourself that this is what practice is.

It will come as no surprise to you that to improve your playing, you have to practice. However, what if I told you that it's not how much practice you do that makes a difference. It's what you do in those practice sessions that determines the outcome of your success.

Most learners confuse practice with playing. There seems to be a general consensus that things improve if you repeat something enough times. Sure, repetition is a part of process, but you have to do it in the right way. Practice should be rewarding, fun and relaxing, shouldn't it? You desire to play and explore your creativity and self-expression; you've got the passion, and now you want to experience the fruits of your labour.

Yet, the reality is that music practice can be frustrating, challenging, and at times, boring. So often, you make progress one day and feel like you take two steps backwards the next. While you dream of playing for your friends and family, the reality is you don't think you are good enough. You tell yourself that you haven't put in enough time, you have no talent, you left it too late. I hate to break it to you, but 80% of learning to play is conquering those fears. It has nothing to do with doing more practice. You have to learn how to practise. Practise is an art form in itself. It requires patience, commitment, awareness and quite frankly, it isn't always fun! However, when done correctly, it's one of the most rewarding things you can do.

In this book, you'll learn how you can make radical progress and play more musically without those extended practice sessions. You'll come to realise that those frustrations can be easily overcome by doing more thinking and less playing. I'll show you how to be more focused and how to set clear musical goals that measure the outcome of your efforts.

You'll learn what to do before you physically practise the first note of a piece and how to conquer the basics. You see, without solid foundations, no amount of practice will give you the desired result. At the heart of all music lies rhythm. Keeping those beats in place makes the music dance and come alive. For many learners, it's the lack of rhythmic precision that lies beneath most problems. Yet, timing is something that you can master when you have the correct methods in place. Once the rhythm dances, your musicality can shine through. It will open a whole new world of musical awareness, allowing your own creativity the opportunity to flourish.

It all starts with bite-sized practice sessions that have a clear focus. When you take only a few bars of music and you experience progress, your motivation soars. You are left wanting more; it's a positive experience that feeds your internal hunger. Experiencing success is what will get you to where you want to be. Musical talent is something that everyone has. The professionals have no more potential than yourself. They've just practised more effectively. It also seems pertinent at this point to mention that adults learn in a very different way to children. Our life experiences, fears and mindset all have an impact on our progress. By understanding how these factors affect us, we can learn to work with them and fulfil our musical potential. Plus, you'll reap the benefit of my holistic methods in other areas of life too. It's never too late to learn, and music is an excellent way of keeping ourselves healthy and our minds engaged.

"I enjoy LMT. There is a holistic approach here that not only adds another dimension in enhancing one's musical journey, but the skills are transferable to other areas in life." **Dolores**

For myself, music has always been a part of my life. If my parents had known that I'd become a professional saxophonist, I'm sure they would have found an alternative way to buy my pram. They married young and had little money. My father had played the saxophone at school, and his precious Conn instrument with the lady figure, was the only thing they had of value. So, when I came along, it was sold and my pram duly bought.

At the young age of three, I remember feeling excited every Friday night as my aunt would come around and teach me recorder. I don't know if I was any good, but I soon progressed to flute at primary school. It was back in the days when music formed part of school assemblies. We used to walk into the hall with classical music playing in the background. James Galway was a particular favourite of the headmistress, so perhaps that's where my love of the flute originates. For that, I have to thank Mrs Henderson and Mrs Hayward from Masefield Primary.

When my sister received a piano one Christmas, I drove my parents mad for lessons. They eventually agreed after I'd spent months teaching myself from a tutor book. Through secondary school, I was lucky enough to have free saxophone lessons. I surrounded myself with music and benefitted from the excellent music department at Canon Slade School. I probably did not show Mr Wilding, the head of music at the time, much gratitude back then, but I want to thank him here for his dedication and passion. It's teachers like Mr Wilding who make an impact on a child which can last forever.

On leaving school, I was talented enough to gain a place at a music college. However, I never truly excelled. My perfectionism, anxiety issues, and lack of confidence held me back. Of course, I didn't know this at the time, but I can see that, in hindsight, I had so much more potential.

At college, you are surrounded by people who are better than you. Your playing is criticised to the nth degree, and any possible thoughts that you could make it as a soloist are stripped away.

With all that said, I wouldn't change it for the world; you see, I wouldn't be where I am today without those experiences. It was shortly after my first term at music college that my outlook on music changed. For reasons I won't go into here, the head of the faculty moved me to an external saxophone tutor, Richard Ingham. I had to travel to his studio each week at my own expense, and I owe a lot to Richard. He taught in a way that was different from every other music teacher I'd had. And I'd had many of them over the years. Richard didn't tell me to practise; he showed me how to practice. From him, I learnt how to listen and hear the beauty of sound. I gained a much deeper understanding of rhythm, and for the first time, I was taught how to practise with a metronome. But most of all, it's thanks to Richard that I gained the confidence to be my unique self.

I remember the reaction of my friends when I told them I wasn't playing any of the standard repertoire works for my final recital. Instead, my program was a diverse mix of pieces chosen to allow my full potential to shine through. Whilst everyone else performed a concerto, my program included a Kenny Gee number, a larger-scale work by a female composer and a contemporary piece with no written notes.

I flourished in my finals and was complimented for my bold and diverse program. It was a significant boost to my confidence and my first experience of doing something against the norm. I mention this as you'll see, throughout this book, there's a common theme which goes against the standard of conventional practice - namely, playing *less* will help you achieve *more*.

Before I left college, I gained a teaching position at a highly academic private school, another step away from the norm of fellow students. To fulfil the role, I had to gain permission from the music college, and I'm thankful to the professors for granting it. For the next 18 years, I thrived in teaching saxophone, to the extent that it became the most popular instrument in the school to learn. I took on the role of musical director for ensembles and formed an international award-winning jazz band and saxophone choir. I went above and beyond to ensure that their musical experience was something that would impact their lives forever. I did copious amounts of fundraising to allow everyone of all financial backgrounds to participate in music tours and lessons.

The kids must have thought that I was mad when I suggested that we take over the school greenhouse to sell hanging baskets. Or the time when we took over the home economics room to make jam. I hasten to add, I couldn't have done that fundraising without the students and the support of their parents. They put their trust in me, and I hope they learnt some valuable life skills.

The success of my efforts saw me feature in the national Girls' Independent School Magazine. The highlights have to include the two performances at Montreux Jazz Festival and my presentation at the World Saxophone Congress. My saxophone quartet at the time made the finals of the prestigious Londiex competition, a feat which was staggering given they were all just 18 and the competition was open to under 30-year-olds.

"How do you do it?" asked my colleague Stephen Martin. "Nobody gets results like you; what is your secret?" My response was simple; I showed people how to get the best results from their practice time. More importantly, I filled my students with confidence and self-belief. Lastly, I encouraged my students to excite younger school members by performing in assemblies regularly. In doing so, they were inspiring the next generation. The latter was most likely the key to my success. Infants and juniors would frequently stop me on the playground to tell me they would play in my band one day. Nothing inspires people more than being part of something bigger. It's why my online academy for adults is called 'Learn Music Together.'

All good things come to an end, though, and as I approached forty years of age, I needed more. I loved to travel, and I wanted to learn more about music. A good friend of mine encouraged me to apply for a role as an examiner at Trinity College, London. At the time, I didn't think I'd stand a chance, mainly because I was too young, and secondly, because I didn't believe the saxophone would be taken seriously enough as a first study instrument. You may laugh at the latter, but it's only in the past decade that the saxophone has earned itself a reputation as a 'proper instrument'. It's thanks to rising stars like Jess Gillam that the saxophone is, at last, being seen as a classical instrument that deserves the same recognition as its traditional orchestral counterparts.

My thoughts were proved wrong, as I successfully gained a place as one of the youngest members of Trinity's examiner panel. Before the Covid 19 pandemic, I spent five exciting years travelling the world and giving feedback to tens of thousands of exam candidates. I was also accepted as an adjudicator for the International Federation of Music Festivals, another role that took me by surprise. Having spent considerable time in India, Thailand, Malaysia, Australia, and Europe, I noticed the difference between adult learners and children. I became fascinated by how adults who were high achievers in their professional fields, doctors, lawyers, CEOs of major companies, would crumble as soon as they walked into the exam room. My heart went out to them, but I could see that their practice methods were mainly to blame. I wanted to help but, at the time, there was little I could do. That was until Covid 19 brought the world to a standstill. For the first time in years, I was back home with little to do. So I set about sharing my knowledge with adults.

Through my Learn Music Together Academy (LMT), I have helped hundreds of adults practise in a smarter way so they can make better progress. My intention with this book is to help thousands more. I know that if you keep on reading and implementing the methods, you too will play better than you have before. You won't have to extend your practice hours, accomplish all your scales, or do endless technical exercises. Instead, you'll achieve strength, speed, agility and more emotion with every note you play by gaining a stronger hold of your musical foundations.

I can tell you that it won't happen overnight, nor is it a journey without its challenges. You will have to go beyond your comfort zone and change your habits. You'll also have to tackle that mindset and those fears that hold so many adults back. However, for those who follow and implement my methods, the rewards are huge.

When you start to learn a new piece every week, the magic begins to happen. There's a new level of excitement that starts to bubble. It spills over as your confidence soars and your motivation propels you forward.

A new 'musical you' emerges with the ability to convey a unique form of self-expression and creativity, one who knows that the greatest gift of music comes in the *giving* and not the *receiving*. You will constantly be gaining momentum and confidence in your playing.

Don't just take my word for it, here's what one of my LMT members has to say:

"I just had my lessons this morning. My teachers are noticing the improvement in my rhythms and how I understand the musical content. I no longer play notes after notes. I am making improvements, but I still feel like a beginner most of the time. That's the wonder aboutlearning. The bigger the challenges, the more mesmerised I have become. It almost like an addiction!" **Elisa**

It's never too late to learn, and the sooner you understand the art of practice, the better. Practice is a habit, and as you probably know, habits are not easy to change. The earlier you begin to implement effective methods, the sooner you'll be fulfilling those dreams and playing with musical integrity.

How this book is organised?
The practise tips you're about to read have proven results. Each chapter provides new secrets to help you achieve more from your practice sessions. My methods will help you strengthen your musical foundations so you can fulfil your potential.

"Play music better" is not a book on theory. Everything I'm going to teach you is based on results from over 25 years of teaching. I've coached students of all ages and abilities, but in the last few years, I've been sharing my knowledge with adult learners through my Learn Music Together Academy. You're going to meet some of those members in this book because I'm a huge fan of teaching from (and by) example. The stories and quotes from this book are all written by real-life people. People you can meet inside the Learn Music Together Academy. They are adults like yourself who want to get better at music.

The book is divided into five sections. Each of these represents the five stages of the musical road map inside the LMT Academy. With every new piece you learn, you should seek to go deeper and deeper in your learning and mastery of your instrument by revisiting each of these five steps.

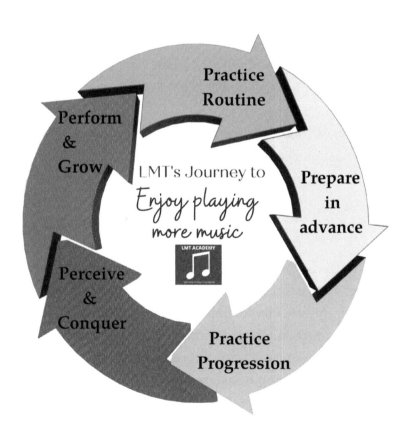

Section One- "Practice and Routines" takes you on a deep journey to "open up to possibility". The aim of this section of the book is to reveal to you why adults and children learn differently. I guide you through some of the challenges that might be holding you back from truly fulfilling your musical potential. I will show you exactly what to do before you practice a new piece and how to plan a sustainable practise routine.

Section Two- "Prepare in Advance" helps you set musical goals to keep you moving forward. I'll teach you how to put action steps in place to ensure you achieve your milestones, and I share the benefits of maintaining a practice diary. These stages are often skipped, yet writing things down and planning your practice in advance will reap you better results, as you'll discover. I'll explain why your body is an extension of your instrument and how breathing affects your muscle movements and ability to play.

Section Three- "Practice Progression" is the meat and potatoes. This is where I share my proven practice methods that will help you make faster and better progress. I'll teach you how to incorporate parts of your piece in your warm-up and the best ways to achieve rhythmic precision. You'll also learn how to structure your practice sessions to improve the retention of the material you've learnt. This is a section of the book that I would encourage you to refer back to time and time again. I've also got some additional training videos and **resources to help.**

Section Four- "Perceive and Conquer" is all about finding solutions to problems. We all have strengths and weaknesses, both in terms of our technical ability and our mindset. I'll share creative ways to help you navigate those hurdles, from struggling with the need to get it "right" to maintaining motivation and momentum. I'll give you lots of ideas to develop your musicality so that you can express yourself through your music. Plus I'll share the best ways to improve your memorisation skills. No matter how effectively you practice, there will inevitably be times when things don't go according to plan. I hope to inspire you in this section of the book with ideas to help you navigate any potential roadblocks.

Section Five -"Perform and Grow" is all about the power of sharing music and how it will enhance your musical enjoyment. I'll show you ways to conquer those anxieties so you can enjoy performing your music confidently to others.

If you follow the formula I reveal in this book; it's highly possible you'll make radical progress and find your musical flow.

Are you ready to get started?

Section 1

Practice and Routines

Chapter 1 - Open Up To Possibility

Before we dive into the practice methods, there's something fundamental to understand. Adults learn in different ways to children, and most of us will need to change our habits to succeed. As adults, we also have to accept that it takes longer to learn a new skill. Unfortunately, our minds and bodies are no longer in the learning phase of life. It takes considerably more time to myelinate neural pathways, but it is possible. You also have to be aware that as adults our thoughts and life experiences influence our beliefs.

Take a look at the six questions below and answer yes or no honestly, to each of them.
1. Do you think you are good enough to perform?
2. If I told you to practise only five notes ascending and descending for the next week, do you think your playing would improve?
3. If I asked you to improvise, would you be comfortable in doing so?
4. Do you get every piece you learn up to the required speed?
5. Do you consider yourself to be good at music?
6. Do you worry that there's not enough time to practise?

Did you answer no to any of the above questions or yes to question 6? If so, you are holding yourself back, and fear is stopping you from fulfilling your potential. You are not alone. Most adults suffer from fear. The Covid 19 pandemic is an example of how fear can suddenly turn your world upside down and change how you behave. Let's take a closer look at why negative responses to those questions make progress more challenging.

Do you think you're good enough to perform?
Adults often tell themselves that they are learning just for fun, and they have no intentions of performing. While that may be true to some extent, you are planting the seed of self-doubt. By telling yourself that you're not good enough to perform, your brain functioning will become consistent with the premise. If we dig deeper into this, there is a fear that we'll fail if we allow ourselves to believe that we could be good enough to perform. It's a common misconception that being a performer means being a professional musician who plays complex music to a large audience on a stage. The reality is that most people want to listen to music that they recognise, can sing along to and feel some kind of connection with. The greatest enjoyment of music comes when you perform for others. The feeling is similar to the one you get when you give a present to someone. For most of us, there's far more joy in the giving than when you receive a gift yourself.

Performing is one of the best ways to improve at any level, as I'll cover in the final chapter. The realisation of this has empowered many of my 'Learn Music Together Academy' members. It's given them a confidence boost and a deeper understanding of the power of music:

"We had our first performance last night. I will pat myself on the back! I nailed the runs, short notes … resolutions … dynamics. All because:

1. *I had each piece analysed to the max.*
2. *I made sure I squared my shoulders and maintained good breathing.*
3. *Kept my focus on the music 100% instead of checking out the audience at times while counting sections of rests. All in all, the practice methods are bearing fruit."* **Sharon**

"What I need to gain is confidence on the piano along with accuracy. I have wanted to play, since I was young, but didn't have an instrument at home growing up. I've had a piano most of my married life but not enough time to concentrate and practice regularly. I now enjoy practicing as I can see progress. Playing sacred music is part of my every morning meditation and devotion time. Thanks for your help, Fiona!" **Esther.**

It could also be the fear of sounding foolish that's holding you back or the fear of being incompetent. So I hope the above words encourage you to start letting go so you can find the courage to perform. I guarantee you have more to gain than lose by brightening up someone's day with a live musical performance.

If I told you to practise only five notes ascending and descending, for the next week, do you think you would improve?

The answer to this should most definitely be a yes. There's something about adults, though; we think we'll go further by cramming more into our practice sessions. One piece isn't enough. Often two pieces aren't enough. One scale's not enough. We layer it up and up and up. Why? Because there's a fear that we don't have enough time, or we're not doing enough to make progress. There's one thing with adults: if something comes easy, we need to make it more complicated. If you work in the world of business, you'll know that the most effective systems are those that are simple. As soon as you get somebody within a company who wants to put a complex system in place, the whole thing goes pear-shaped. Simple is always effective. However, the flip side of that coin is that adults don't like change. *There's a comfort within familiarity, and even when a process makes sense, we often put up a resistance to change.* I want you to write that last sentence down and as you read on, refer to it regularly.

If I asked you to improvise, would you be happy to do so?

I would surmise that most readers who study classical music answered no. If you are a jazz player, I hope you said yes. Guitarists also tend to be more flexible and don't mind playing around with a few chords. But if you play classical piano, you probably answered with an outright 'no, that's not for me.' If this is you, I want you to know that it's another misconception which leads us to such objections. Many people associate improvisation with Jazz, and therefore it's not something classical players can or need to do. We conjure up an image of a fantastic musician improvising with flair and creativity that's way beyond our limits. But actually, improvisation is freedom within the music. It's just freedom to make sound and express your emotion without having sheet music in front of you. It's the fear of inadequacy or failure that causes you to resist even having a go. And if it makes you feel better, even the best improvisers are not truly authentic. They have their favourite riffs and motifs that have become their signature style.

Do you get every piece you learn up to the required speed?
If you answered no to this, well, you should be doing so! Again this comes back to the fear of wasting time—fear of not making progress quickly enough. We might tell ourselves,

'I could actually achieve that if I did a bit more practice. I haven't got time to do that. So I'm going to move on, but I could do it if necessary.'

However, you aren't doing that practice, and therefore you're not fulfilling the technical requirements. You are not only compromising the development of your technique, but you are also holding yourself back musically. Playing at the required tempo is one of the musical elements necessary to fulfil the character of a piece. For example, a waltz should have a one in a bar feeling; without it, the playing sounds more pedestrian than dance-like.

Do you consider yourself to be not very good at music?

For many, these types of thoughts stem back to education. School reports today tend to put a more positive spin on things. Still, not that long ago, it was perfectly acceptable to be told that you weren't very good at whatever subject. Such statements are powerful and have a long-lasting effect. They often stay with us throughout adulthood disguised as the fear of failure. Or perhaps even more debilitating is the fear of being foolish. If you tell yourself, *'I am good at music'*, then it's almost like you've got everything to prove. Hence, we tell ourselves the opposite so as not to fail. The truth is everybody has the potential to be good at music. We all have the ability to play musical instruments; you just have to nurture the skills. As David Coyle explains in his book, 'The Talent Code'

"Skill is myelin insulation that wraps neural circuits, and that grows according to certain signals."

Do you worry that there's not enough time to practice?

This one is a favourite amongst learners, and it's a good contender for first place when it comes to blocking progress. The western culture of practice tells us that you need to do hours and hours of practice to be good at anything. You may have read the suggestions by people like Malcolm Gladwell that it takes ten thousand hours of practice to master a skill. However, don't be disheartened. The adult enthusiast who wants to play for pleasure at a decent level, does not need to do that much daily practice in order to make incredible progress. Even five minutes, every day, doing something such as clapping rhythms, is beneficial. So often, it's the thought that you haven't got enough time that prevents you from getting started. The fear of not knowing where to begin can also hold you back. It's all too easy to spend time procrastinating and achieve very little. Of course, at the other end of the spectrum, perfectionists battle with nothing ever being good enough. The latter I am completely familiar with as I'm a recovering perfectionist myself.

We all have fears, and overcoming them or learning to address them is the first step to taking progressive steps forward. So as you read on, I want to encourage you to be aware of any fears that are holding you back and see if you can let go of them as you continue through this book.

Chapter 2 - Adults Learn Differently From Children

Most advice on the internet, and within tutor books, doesn't consider that adults learn differently from children. Adults often make the most challenging of students for the reasons that I'm about to discuss. For a start, they judge themselves by the outcome. In many ways, this process starts when you leave school. Most students around the world have to pass exams to gain a place at college or university. It's often the first real experience of judging by an outcome. When you sit these exams, you either pass or fail, which is detrimental in specific subjects such as maths. Most educational systems will tell you that, you are unlikely to get a job without those qualifications.

When we enter the workplace, promotion and careers are often related to the outcome of an interview or how successfully you fulfil a role. As we get older, we encounter more experiences that are judged by the results of our efforts.

When adults practise music, they judge their progress by how well they can play a piece. Rarely do they look at what they've learnt or accomplished in the process. Children, on the other hand, are the opposite. They adapt throughout the process. The best example I can give you is of a child learning to walk. When a child takes their first steps, they wobble and fall down constantly. However, they don't give in. When they fall, they giggle and then bounce straight back up and have another go. They make a few minor adjustments and try again. They're probably not aware of the changes, but it doesn't take long before they're running so fast you can't keep up.

When it comes to learning any skill, adults often set unrealistic expectations; it's why so many people have gym memberships that they never use. In my 'Effective Practice' masterclass, I ask people to choose a piece they think they can learn in one week, and I'm always astounded by the advanced works that land in my inbox. I'm interested right now in what piece you'd choose, so do let me know by getting in touch.

Children usually have their expectations outlined for them, by school teachers or parents. If they do have an opportunity to set their own, they often underestimate what they can achieve. It's far more fun when you set your own goals and experience success every time you practice.

The next difference between adults and children is a *biggie* and one which you have to accept. Adults learn at a slower pace. That's a scientific fact and one you have no control over, I'm afraid. Children are in what's called the *learning phase* of life. They're like sponges. They absorb *everything.* So if you've got children or grandchildren who are learning to play an instrument, and they are making way better progress than you, that's because they're in the learning phase of life. It can often take a child only a few years to become reasonably proficient at playing an instrument, whereas, for adults, you can at least double the time required. As we get older, the ability to build myelin decreases, which is why the world's best players mostly started at a young age. I'll talk more about myelin in chapter 8, but for now know that myelin is a fat that wraps around the nerve fibres. Think of it like the insulation foam you put around copper piping to protect it. Myelin optimises the speed and accuracy of 'the wires' within our nervous system. Simply put, the more myelin you acquire, the better you can do that action. That doesn't mean that you can't become proficient as an adult learner. We are capable of producing myelin no matter how old we are, but the process does slow down. So let go and don't allow yourself to feel like you are behind and resist the temptation of comparing yourself to others.

Often, adults are overly serious in their learning and they lack confidence. It might be that you've heavily invested in your instrument or lessons. Perhaps it's something you've always wanted to do, so you take it very seriously when the opportunity arises. Practise sessions can become very intense and are often devoid of any creativity. Children, on the other hand, like to have fun when they learn. Creativity and laughter are things which come naturally to them, and these things facilitate and promote their learning. Similarly, when adults relax more in their learning, they progress much further.

I've already mentioned that adults live in fear. Young children are entirely the opposite. They are fearless, which is why baby manufacturers make a fortune. Parents purchase all sorts of safety items to modify the home and protect their child as they've yet to experience or understand what fear is. And when you don't have fear, you have freedom.

Our reactions to situations are often much more defensive as adults. For the most part, adults hate being told that they are doing something wrong. In these situations, most people will try to defend their current actions. Some may go as far as to argue a point just to start an entertaining debate. It's their way of creating a diversion from admitting the error of their ways. Children are rarely that confrontational. They are used to teachers addressing their mistakes and will often ask questions for guidance or help. They would be more inquisitive about finding a solution to their problem.

For the most part, children follow instructions. While their teachers would love them to take the initiative, they rarely do more or less than the directions given. Adults are often the opposite and like to do things their way. We tend to take instructions and put our own little twist on things. We just can't help ourselves. We also like to do more research and look into something far deeper than is necessary. While this is not always a bad thing, it can prevent us from taking action.

Throughout life, our experiences can have a profound effect on our reactions. So often, it's how we respond in our practice that makes a difference. We take action based on our thoughts and feelings. Patience and resilience are two essential ingredients that you need in abundance if you want to learn to play an instrument well. Adults can, at times, throw in the towel too soon or let their frustrations take over. An excellent example of this is in the field of technology. So many adults think that they are not good with technology, but this is not necessarily true. If you are interested enough and take the time to practice, you will succeed. You are most likely going too fast, clicking things without thinking, and then panicking because something isn't working. Frustration soon builds, and then you quit without really allowing yourself to learn.

Maybe you've had a bad experience with using a computer. Perhaps you found it difficult and weren't willing to give it a fair chance. Unfortunately, I'm of that generation where computers didn't exist when I was at school. Hence I'm self-taught, but I have now built an online program, so if I can do it you can too. The same goes for music practice.

Before we move on, throughout this book I will be asking you to form new habits, which is always a challenge. Adults often don't like change. (Did you write that down in chapter 1?) We also tend to learn things independently, whereas children learn best in a social learning environment. They have continuous support from teachers, friends, and other students. Surrounding yourself with a network of people is going to help you form new habits. Being part of a group of like-minded people is a sure way to make progress, so if you haven't yet joined my community, here's your personal invitation. Hop on over and introduce yourself.

Chapter 3 – A Quick Win

Learning an instrument is not easy, and there aren't many tips that reap instant results. However, what I'm about to share will make a huge difference to your progress. So often, learners dive straight into the playing without any preparation. Mistakes happen because they have so much to think about, such as reading the notes, finding the finger combinations, counting the rhythms, making a good sound, etc. These mistakes then become more and more challenging to put right later.

You can get ahead in your practice and learn so much by writing things on your music. These markings raise your awareness and heighten your concentration. They also help your brain and memory digest the information, making it easier to achieve more accuracy when you begin practising the notes.

I want to encourage you to invest quality time in preparing your music by sharing Elisa's story. Elisa has been a member of my Learn Music Together Academy for six months now. She initially participated in my 'Learn the Secret to Effective Practice' masterclass. Here is what she wrote after the masterclass had finished:

"I took away many things from the masterclass. How to analyse a piece of music before actually learning - it is so helpful. I know all about scales etc. But I never thought about

'recognising' patterns in the music. It is way more interesting than just starting from the beginning. There are so many other tips. It's a wonderful masterclass. Thank you, Fiona."

Over the past six months inside 'Learn Music Together,' Elisa has been making fantastic progress. She has really taken to analysing her music. She's also developed a keen ear for listening and now spends much more time preparing her music. Recently Elisa attended a chamber string orchestra workshop and had only three weeks to learn two Vivaldi concertos and three other pieces. She put my practice tips into action, starting with looking through the music, then moving on to analysing and marking all the key signatures and accidentals.

Elisa focused on the trickiest parts first and regularly noted down what she would do to make progress in her practice diary. But most of all, Elisa spent lots of time listening to the music on YouTube and clapping out the rhythms. The last sentence is an important tip to note. It's common for adult learners to think they can only make progress when they practise on an instrument, which isn't the case. There are many ways to practise without playing. For Elisa it was not possible to play her cello, as her bow had broken, and she had sent it away to be fixed. This is what she wrote on the Learn Music Together Forum:

"No instrument? No problema ... practice can still go on ... I just listen and do more listening and more clapping. Now ten days later
... I have managed all of the pieces at 80% of the tempo. I could never have done that before joining LMT".

So often, learners dive straight in and start practising the notes without even looking through the music. In contrast, professional musicians spend a considerable amount of time studying their scores and working out what they need to focus on in their practice sessions.

Analysing their performance is something elite sportspeople do too. They spend copious amounts of time with their coaches, looking for ways to improve their golf swing, swim stroke, or backhand etc. No matter what level you are at, raising your awareness through analysation helps.

When you study your music, you need to highlight anything that will help your brain process information. In doing so, you'll bring something to your attention before you practice. Hence, when you arrive at that point in the music, you are much less likely to make errors. It makes what you are learning more accessible and speeds up the whole process. So who wouldn't want to do that? Your markings will help you focus your attention, increase your awareness, and enable you to practise more mindfully. It also helps structure your practice sessions. All of these elements are important if you're going to make consistent progress.

What should you write on your music?

If you're a beginner, start with some simple things. As you progress musically, your markings will become more in-depth. One of the most common errors I see from students is forgetting the key signature when they practise. You can avoid making this mistake by highlighting all the sharps, flats, and necessary accidentals on the score.

Now, I can hear some people saying, well, that's cheating. I should be able to remember them, or that's not going to help my sight-reading. However, it's simply not true. Highlighting sharps and flats doesn't mean that you won't be able to remember them in the future if you're sight-reading a piece. It is completely the opposite; it makes you much more mindful. You will become accustomed to checking the key signature and looking for accidentals in the music. Missing accidentals which last for the whole bar is another common error amongst learners. In my twenty plus years of teaching, I've never had a student struggle with remembering key signatures further down the line because they highlighted them. Lots of professional musicians mark up their music prior to rehearsals. So, while they might not circle everything, they'll always put in any accidentals that they're likely to miss. So don't be afraid to take out a highlighter pen and get colouring in!

From Max Reger, Romanze in G, bars 16-21

If you have an objection to using a highlighter pen on your music, and I know some of you will - my mother was a librarian, and she's horrified by how I fold corners of books and highlight text - so I understand that this is a challenge for some. The good news is there are ways you can work around this. If you own a copy of the book, the easiest one is to photocopy the music you are learning. That way, you can highlight away without worrying that you'll destroy the book.

A little side note here, please remember not to share music that's in copyright with others. Not only is it illegal, but you are also depriving composers of their income. Perhaps an even better solution, because you can remove it if you make a mistake, is to purchase some highlighter tape. It's removable, so that you can reuse it time and time again.

Mark on any repetition
Within most music, there are bars, phrases and motifs that repeat. Inexperienced learners often don't identify these.

31

When you start at the beginning of the piece and work your way down, you don't notice which sections of the music are repeated. Hence, you waste time working through bars that you've already practised. By highlighting anything that is the same, it cuts down your workload. Plus you'll be engaging the cognitive side of the brain, which will help you memorise the music in the future.

Task!

Study your piece carefully and highlight any part that repeats. You'll most likely need a few colours so that you can colour code those bars and identify them instantly.

As you progress along your musical journey, you'll discover that composers often use musical forms and melodic devices to compose. Rondo form, for example, has a phrase or a section that keeps repeating, with new ideas in between. Songs often have a bridge passage, and a classical Minuet regularly repeats the first section at the end. The sections within a piece often modulate (change key) and, as your understanding of music develops, you'll identify key changes more easily. Most modulations are to closely related keys, such as the relative minor, the dominant (V) or the subdominant (IV).

Highlight any repetition and scale patterns

From Telemann, Fantasia in C major TWV 33.14, Gavotte

33

Mark on any scale patterns

It's common to practice scales in your warm-up, but I'm always surprised by how many learners will practice patterns that are unrelated to the piece that they are learning. Why spend time practising G major if your music is in Bb major? Most music is composed using scale patterns. However, these patterns are often incomplete, which makes them harder to identify. They could be notes from arpeggios that are not in order, fragments of scales, common chord patterns or a motif. Look closely through your music as they might not begin on the tonic note (the first note). Highlight and label any patterns that you can find.

Pattern recognition is one of the most helpful ways that you can make progress. In the world of science, they call it chunking. It's something you already do when you read words on a page. Read the sentence below:

'The cat sat on the mat.'

There are 3 chunks in that sentence which your brain sees as patterns.

| The Cat | sat on | the mat |

If I space the letters differently in that phrase, it becomes more challenging to read.

It's the same in music. If you can see the patterns, you'll be able to play them more easily. *Patterns can be rhythmical as well as notational.* Once you've highlighted the patterns in your music you can use those to warm-up. So instead of playing any random scale, practice the scales that *relate* to the piece you are learning.

Rhythms

Playing with rhythmical precision will transform your music, but getting to that stage isn't easy. Writing the counts on your piece will ensure that you are thinking about the timing from day one. A bar of crotchets (quarter notes) for a beginner can be complex, so don't under estimate the value of putting the beats on the score. I like to use words for shorter note lengths – more of that later.

When it comes to complicated subdivisions, in the early stages of your practise, I would suggest putting vertical lines where the main beats fall, and, subdivide the bar into smaller

35

divisions. Those vertical lines will help you align the beats with a metronome.

From I. Albeniz, Tango in D, bars 1-4

Fingering
Beginner books tend to write on all the necessary fingering, but this becomes less so as you progress. Think about where you are likely to make a mistake if you don't remember to stretch a finger, for example, on the piano or cross your thumb under at the right time. Resist the temptation to play the piece when you are doing this, as you don't want to make mistakes. If need be, play the notes as long notes to help you work out the best fingering combinations. Then make a note on your music.

There are often several fingering options for notes on specific instruments. For example, there are five ways to play B flat on a saxophone, yet many people only utilise one. Brass players might find it helpful to write on the valve positions for some notes, and string players may want to consider the string positions. You want to practice with the same fingering every time. So writing it on the music score, of course, makes that job so much easier.

Breath Marks

If you play a wind or brass instrument, I recommend marking on the music where you will breathe. Sing through the phrases, and listen to a recording to get some ideas. Don't tell yourself you can't sing, have a go; your goal is to work out the most musical place to take a breath.

If you need a little guidance, a general rule is to breathe after a longer note value. If your piece begins with an anacrusis (an upbeat), the next phrase will most likely do so too. Hence you'll also need to breathe before that pickup and not on the bar line.

Bowing Marks

String players should consider adding bowing marks. Putting such markings in place will help you achieve more consistency in your practice and encourage you to be more mindful of the actions that you need to take.

Phrasing

If you are a beginner, you may not know what phrasing means, but think of it as a musical sentence. Phrases are often the same length and begin in a similar way. More often than not, they are two or four bars in length. When analysing your music, start by comparing bars 1 and 5 to see if there are any similarities. If not, try bars 1 and 3. More advanced players should be competent enough to mark on the phrases, but you can find more detail in chapter 18, if you need a helping hand.

Mark on the phrasing, breath or bowing marks

From Tchaikovsky, Op.39 Children's Album, No 16 bars 1-8

Considerations for More Advanced Players

There are so many things that you could make notes about before you begin learning a new piece. Here are a few ideas:

- Does the music follow a structure, such as Sonata form? If so, can you mark on the exposition, the development section and the recapitulation?

- Can you make a note of any keys the piece modulates to or goes through?
- If you are playing or singing a song, is there a bridge passage or a key change for any of the verses?
- You can write down your musical thoughts and intentions.
- How much vibrato or rubato will you deploy? Are there any pitch bends that you will add?
- What is the character or mood of that section? How will you communicate that to your audience?
- Do you need to add other dynamic shades?
- What should the textural balance of the phrase be, is there any motif that you need to bring to the fore?

Whatever level you are working at, analysing the music will help you tie together musical theory and how that works in practice. Don't worry if you can't write everything that I have mentioned on your score. Even writing, just one of these things, will help you make better progress.

When you can identify patterns such as arpeggios or chords and make notes about your musical intentions, it makes learning so much easier. Knowing where the phrases start and end means you'll play with more musicality from day one.
Marking all the sharps/ flats and accidentals before you practice means you're much less likely to play a wrong note.
You will also benefit from listening to the piece. So find a good recording to listen to regularly. By listening, you are opening

up your creative side and learning to hear the notes before you play them.

Thinking of skipping this step?

Writing on your music is an elementary step. People who fail to play with a high degree of accuracy in their practice, often fail to take analysing their music seriously. That's their first and most fundamental mistake.

Marking up your score allows you to make progress quicker with minimal effort. Failing to analyse your music will likely lead to errors in pitch, rhythm, fingering and error pathways (more on those to come) which are hard to correct.

Here are a few quotes from people who have followed my effective practice roadmap to successfully achieve greater accuracy and fluency in their playing.

"Feel good. Did some sight reading today and went back to basics, highlighted the key signatures throughout my pieces, played scales and arpeggios, then clapped the rhythm before playing. Much better results. Thanks." **Nicky Moore.**

"Fiona I'm excited to share that I started a new piece for my piano lesson. I marked things to remember on the music with highlighters, analysed which measures repeated. Then, in my daily journal, for morning and afternoon practice, I noted what measures I worked on with the metronome. I'm thrilled as it's going well! ..." **Bev.**

Section 2

Prepare Before Practice

Chapter 4 - Your Practice Routine

Practice is a skill and an art form in itself. While many adult learners are enthusiastic, they often confuse playing with practising. Keen beginners and even more advanced players tend to expect too much from themselves, and dare I say it, they can be over-ambitious.

The ideal way to achieve consistency and accomplish more when you practice is to keep to a *realistic* schedule.
I regularly post the question *'How Much Practice do you do?'* on my Facebook Page, **Musician in the Making,** and the answers nearly always fall one of two ways. The first category highlight their own shortcomings (I don't do enough practice / I struggle to find the time to practise), whilst the second enters into a kind of egotistical game of who can claim they do the most.

Consistency is vital when it comes to practice. Extended practice sessions at the weekend to make up for missed sessions during the week are *ineffective.* You need to create a routine which you can easily incorporate into your everyday life. This chapter will cover how much practice time you should do and provide a few suggestions for those whom finding or scheduling time is an issue.

Before I go any further, it's essential to understand the difference between playing and practise. Those who claim to practise for hours within one session are not being true to themselves. Practise should be like an intense workout. There should be a clear focus within your session and a way to measure your progress. You should never play the whole piece through until you know that you can play every bar. Instead, you should focus on a bite-sized section of music and set specific goals. You should be aware of everything you do and similarly, you should do everything with intention.

Playing, on the other hand, is the fun part. At the end of your practice is the time to enjoy playing some music that you can already play. **Don't, however, play the piece that you are currently learning.**

Why short sessions lead to better progress.
You've probably experienced going through the motions of practising when your mind is elsewhere. Perhaps you were thinking about cooking dinner or that email that needs a response. It happens to us all. Everybody's mind starts to wander after approximately 15 minutes of doing a task. Sure we can train ourselves to focus for longer, but you should always take a break after no more than 30 minutes. Hence, to achieve more when you practice, take regular breaks and do shorter sessions *more frequently.*

There is an overwhelming amount of scientific research which proves that shorter practice sessions with regular breaks speed up the learning process. The studies also show that 'spaced learning' improves your retention.

I recommend two practice sessions a day of around 20 minutes each.

Ideally, you want to put a few hours' break between them. If you are practising for much longer than this, you are probably working way harder than necessary and not reaping the benefits. Plus, you are unlikely to retain as much of the information.

If you are a more advanced player, you can increase the amount of 20 minute practice sessions. However, you should practice different sections of music in each session, take a break every 20 minutes, and a much longer break after three sessions.

Practising less, yet still making more progress, is often challenging for people to understand. It seems counterintuitive, right? Our culture of practice so often seems to push the concept that more practice automatically means more improvement. For many learners, it's fear that drives you to this way of thinking. Our subconscious mind tells us that there's too much to learn, so we better practice more. Many learners often worry that they'll forget something if they don't play it every day even when they have experienced the opposite. Have you ever improved or least not got any worse when you've been unable to practice for a few days?

Scientific research tells us the opposite, that is, that breaks are important for a number of reasons.

Why breaks are essential.

You need to take regular breaks to ensure you remain entirely focused during your practice. Frequent breaks also speed up the learning process. Without going into an in-depth science lesson, breaks are necessary for a process called long term potentiation to happen. For our brains to carry out a complex process such as playing an instrument, the neurons (information messengers in our brain) have to connect and undergo construction. Now some neurons need longer to complete this process than others. Those neurons can only complete the construction process if we rest. When we take a break, the brain also moves the information to a more stable place, making the action easier when we try it again later. As a guide, the more complex the music passage is, the more space you should leave before practising it again. Think days rather than hours in this case.

Sleep also has a magical part to play. When we sleep, the brain keeps working. Research has shown that those who get less than 8 hours sleep per night are compromising the learning process. The brain consolidates our memories in the last 2 hours of sleep (hours 7 and 8). It moves the information into even more stable storage and creates space to make new memories. If you want to learn more about the importance of sleep, I highly recommend that you read the book 'Why we Sleep' by Matthew Walker. Here are a couple of quotes from his book:

"... Sleep six hours or less and you are shortchanging the brain of a learning restoration benefit that is normally performed by sleep spindles."

"... The second benefit of sleep for memory comes after learning, one that effectively clicks the 'save' button on those newly created files. In doing so, sleep protects newly acquired information, affording immunity against forgetting."

To get the most out of your sessions, you want to work through the material you practice on an expanding schedule, one which includes short breaks initially and longer breaks as you progress. I'll cover more on this in section 3 of the book.

Planning your practice.

When planning your practice routine bear in mind that we are creatures of habit. If you practice at the same time each day and associate your sessions with an event, you'll find it easier to establish and maintain a routine. An event is something you do regularly, such as eating breakfast or returning home from work.

Tip!

To achieve more when you practice, take regular breaks and do shorter sessions more frequently.

Don't limit yourself by creating excuses; you only need to find 15 minutes twice a day. It's also worth noting that not all of your practice sessions need to involve physically playing your instrument. There are plenty of things you can do while commuting or on your lunch break that will help you make progress.

If you lack motivation, it's most likely due to feeling overwhelmed or not experiencing consistent progress. I hope the list below provides you with a new burst of enthusiasm to get started. However, be under no illusion that practising is something you'll always want to do. Habits are not easy to form. There will be times when you will need to make yourself take action, especially in the early stages. Once you start your new regime and get results, self-motivation becomes so much easier.

Planning Tips
1. Schedule practice times for the week in advance. Aim to keep as many of your practice sessions at the same time each day.
2. Find a good quote to motivate you and keep it on your music stand or as a screensaver.
3. Make a list of things you can do to practice without your instrument, e.g. blog posts to read, YouTube channels, podcasts, books, worksheet, clapping exercises etc.
4. Divide your piece into bite-size sections and allocate one to every practice session.
5. Plan your practice sessions, in detail, ahead of time.

6. Be clear on what piece, scale, area of technique you are focusing on for the day / week / month.
7. Set goals, both short term and long term.
8. Keep a practice diary.

Practice Routine Planning Exercise

"If you add a little to a little and do this often, soon the little will become great."

For some, planning comes easy, but for others, it can be challenging. The following planning exercise will help you plan a practice routine that works for you. We all have things that we need to do, such as going to work, preparing and eating meals, but we also have some things that we choose to do, like watching television and practising our instrument.

Write a list of things you have to do each day and give specific start and end times. Then answer the questions below to help you find two, 15-minute practice sessions per day.

Could you fit some practice in before you leave the house?	Yes / No
Can you do some practice on your commute to work?	Yes / No
Could you do some practice, without your instrument, in your lunch break?	Yes / No
Could you do some practice before dinner?	Yes / No

Can you fit in a 15-minute practice session in the evening	Yes / No
Is there a set time you can practice each weekend?	Yes / No

People are often surprised having done this exercise how much spare time they actually have. Look at everything you've written down and decide when you are going to practice each day.

Ideally, you want two 20 minute sessions 6 days a week.

In a small minority of cases, this may not be possible. I recently had an LMT member (Jonathan) who worked away from home regularly as an Events Manager. He stayed in hotels, so practising his saxophone wasn't an option. As I explained to Jonathan, *'you have to plan a routine that will work for you'*, which means getting creative with your practice methods. The biggest mindset change for Jonathan was understanding that he could practise and make progress *without his saxophone*. I'm not suggesting for a moment that this is an ideal situation, but in Jonathan's case, it was the only option. I presented a list of ideas to him so that he could establish a routine that works. These included breathing exercises, clapping exercises, and things he could do to develop his listening skills.

Whether you are in a similar situation or not, practising without your instrument is time well spent. The list below gives you a few ideas, and you'll read later in the book how *mindful* practice strengthens your *physical* practice.

How do you practice away from your instrument?

For those who are short of practice time or can't get to their instruments, there are several things that you can do to help you make progress.

1. You can tap out the beat to any music you listen to during the day.
2. Visualise the music you are learning. Can you talk your way through the notes and patterns?
3. Can you talk through the fingering patterns? Are there any areas of uncertainty or a finger that is particularly weak? Can you do some finger isolation exercises?
4. You could create a mind map to help you learn individual sections or the whole piece.
5. Make a recordings comparison of the piece that you are practising. What are the differences, what do you like about the performance? What do you not like?
6. Practise some ear tests; there are plenty of apps and YouTube channels that can help.
7. Practise some breathing exercises to increase awareness of being mindful or strengthen your abdominal muscles.
8. You can study your music by having a picture on your phone, clap out the rhythms, sing the melody.
9. Do some finger coordination exercises.

10. Read a blog post - If you haven't already done so, check out the posts on Learn Music together.com
11. Listen to a podcast on music.
12. Watch a film related to music, such as Howard Goodall's, 'The Story of Music' available on YouTube.
13. Analyse the music that you are practising. Highlight the key signature, chord sequences, mark on the phrase structure and your musical intentions.
14. Say the letter names or fingering patterns to help learn scales.
15. Practice reading note names using an app or flashcards.
16. Do some mental practice (more on that later in the book).

I hope these suggestions get the creative juices flowing and provide you with a few ideas.

Choosing Suitable Music to Practice.

Most adult learners are over-ambitious in their music choices. While tutor books are a great place to start, you need to learn supplementary pieces along the way to consolidate each step. Far too often, tutor books teach you something new on every page. At first, we keep up well, but it doesn't take long before we are just learning in a rote or in a 'parrot fashion' way. Often you can listen to the music and learn by copying. While this gives you the desired result of playing a piece, it doesn't necessarily provide you with transferrable skills to apply to the next thing you learn.

'Many musicians are fixated on complex elements that they fail to spend enough time on the basics.' **Kenny Werner**

The depth of understanding diminishes, and your progress becomes slower and slower. Without a solid grasp of the basics, you will always get to a point where progress seems to reach a plateau.

'If you don't stay with the material long enough for it to become comfortable, you'll find that it doesn't stay with you.'

Kenny Werner

Until you've mastered the basics, you want to focus on one piece at a time. Choose music that you can learn in one week. Regardless of what level you are at, you should be able to play the piece to a reasonable standard, perhaps below tempo, in 7 days. If it's taking you much longer, you haven't got a good grasp of the basics. You probably need to work on your rhythmic skills, your sight-reading ability and your technique. Furthermore, your practice methods need work, and you need to practice more holistically.

'The wise musicians are those who play what they can master.'

Duke Ellington

It's also essential to choose a diverse range of styles when looking for music to practice. Adults tend to focus on music that they want to learn, particularly if they are not under the guidance of a teacher. Encompassing a more comprehensive range of styles will ensure that you develop all aspects of technique. It will open your creative mind further and expand your musical influences. You'll start to notice similarities across various genres and learn new rhythmic patterns. If you are in need of inspiration, examination books often provide a good selection of pieces. Remember you don't have to prepare or take an exam to work through the material in such books.

Side Note

If you are preparing for an examination, audition or concert recital, it will take you longer than a week to elevate your chosen pieces to the required standard. However, my point here is that far too many people punch way above their level. You should always be striving for accuracy in a musical way. If you are focused entirely on playing the right notes in the right place, you will not have the headspace to express your musical intentions.

It's also far more enjoyable when you make quick progress. Nothing is worse for motivation than struggling for months, trying to accomplish a piece to a mediocre standard. Once you've engrained the mistakes, it's almost impossible to eliminate them, and there's little satisfaction when progress is slow. When you regularly accomplish one new piece per week, progress, motivation and enthusiasm are easy to fuel. Each practice you take a bite-size portion of music, you practise and experience progress, this in turn makes you feel good. The *success of your efforts* then gives you the motivation and drive to do more. It's a cycle which continually gains momentum and it's infectious.

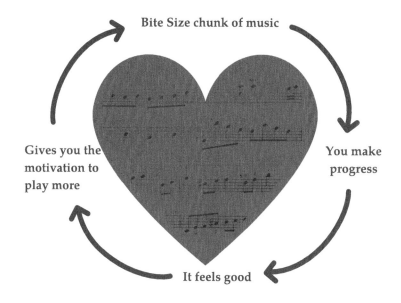

Listen to the piece a lot.

The more you listen to music, the more you'll learn. Before practising a new piece of music, it's hugely beneficial to listen to the piece repeatedly before learning the notes. Plus, it's something that you can do while doing other things. Long gone are the days when you had to search for a professional recording in a record store. YouTube, Spotify, Apple Music, Google downloads, Ask Alexa, and Soundcloud are all resources that you can use through the internet. There are so many places these days where you can go download music, which makes finding recordings so accessible. You'll find that most of the pieces you choose to learn will be available to listen to *free of charge,* which is wonderful.

YouTube is a great place to start when searching for a recording. Type in the search bar the name of the piece and the composer. You can also add your instrument if the original music was composed for something else. You may need to play around with the search words, depending upon how well known your piece is. If you don't get any results from YouTube, try a google search, but add mp3 after the title and composer. If possible, take the time to explore several recordings of the piece and find an outstanding performance.

When recordings aren't available, you have to practice hearing the music internally, which is another skill that needs developing. So make life easier for yourself, there's so much music available for you to learn, choose something that you can listen to.

Historical or Contextual Research
Understanding the historical context of the piece you are learning will help you realise the composer's intentions. You'll discover that composers have compositional styles that they favour. The more you do this, the more you'll learn about form, texture, and similarities between musical periods. Start by researching the composer and other pieces they've written. See if you can find out why they composed the piece and whether it was intended for any purpose. Maybe listen to

some of their other compositions and see how they compare to the piece you are learning.

Find out more about the title, particularly if it's something specific like a Nocturne or a Gavotte. These generic titles give you an insight into the piece's character, but only if you understand what they are.

If you're learning a song, take the time to read through the words. Ask yourself how the character of the music conveys the story. Was the song written about someone or a life event? Why did the artist write the song? There's so much information out there on the internet, and it's all at your fingertips. The more time you spend researching, the more you'll start to recognise the characteristics that composers use in their writing.

Your Practice Space
Now in the perfect world, we'd all have a music room that no one else would use, but the reality is most people have to practice in a space that's shared with others. Having an area with everything you need is the first step to making the most of your practice sessions. Find a space where you can practice every day, free from distractions. We'll come to planning a routine shortly, but it's a good idea to consider how others use the space when planning your routine. Ideally, you will want to have the room to yourself during your practice sessions.

Free the Clutter, Free the Mind

Clutter is one of the worst forms of distraction, and it isn't good for the soul. Over a third of your brain is dedicated to processing visual information, which is far more than that which supports sound or movement. Your eyes will undoubtedly be distracted by the clutter, which means you'll be less focused during your practice.

If your practice space is a mess right now, *put down this book and tidy up*. Put away those books and the sheet music you are no longer using. Eliminate anything that may be a distraction to you during your practice, especially electronic devices and mobile phones. Put them on flight mode if you need to use any Apps. You should only have the following to hand:

Practice Space Checklist
• Sheet music that you are currently practicing
• Pencil & highlighter
• Rubber (eraser)
• Metronome
• Music Practice Diary
• Practice Plan
• Instrument and Stand
• Tuning machine
• Clock
• Manuscript paper

Before you move on to the next chapter, here's a quick checklist of things to have in place.

1. A tidy practice space with everything that you will need close by .
2. A practice routine that consists of two 20 minute sessions per day.
3. A list of ideas for things you can do without your instrument.
4. A piece to practice of the appropriate standard for your level, that you can learn in one week.

If you've ticked off all the above, it's now time to look at setting yourself some musical goals to help structure your practice sessions effectively.

Chapter 5 - Musical Goals

Whether you want to kick start a new piece with greater intentions, prepare for a concert, or examination, setting musical goals will help you move forward.

You need to formulate any goals you set in a measurable way that helps you create habits. Simply stating a few goals is unlikely to work. It's why so many new year resolutions are broken within a few weeks or even days because:

"Goals poorly formulated are goals easily forgotten."

Michael Hyatt

In this section, I'll share my tips so that you can 'Make it Happen' when it comes to planning and achieving your musical goals. We can all have great plans and act with the best of intentions, but we often have to change our habits to succeed.

What are Habits?

Habits are decisions and actions that we do regularly. Good practice habits are essential to establish as we rely on them when anxious or stressed. It's important to try and shape our habits mindfully so that they help us make progress.

Good habits support us, while bad habits make situations worse.

Habits have a tremendous role to play in promoting intellectual growth. They help us become consistent and ensure that we make progress.

Progress begins when we achieve clarity on where we are.

Established habits are hard to change because they take place in our subconscious. We often do things without thinking about them. For example, in the practice room, many learners fail to stop as soon as they make a mistake. They don't intend to carry on, but before they realise, they've played the next couple of notes before stopping. Not only does this waste time during practice, but more importantly, it strengthens an incorrect pathway making it harder to achieve accuracy later. The first step in establishing or changing a habit is to create milestones to help you measure your progress.

What are Milestones?
Milestones are action steps that help us move forwards towards our goals, while good habits help us achieve our milestones. Such achievements are essential as they provide the motivation and direction to ensure that we are on track to accomplishing our goals. We also need to celebrate our milestones as it helps us continually succeed and gain results. So often, our goals fail because we don't honestly believe that we can achieve them. The older we get, the less likely we are to succeed. We tend to have preconceptions formed from past experiences that influence our current mindset. The results of past failings remain in our subconscious minds. Most of us

have a little voice in our heads that loves nothing better than to plant the seeds of self-doubt.

Everyone is more than capable of achieving their goals if they believe in themselves. That doesn't mean it will be easy or that we'll know *how* we will accomplish them. Every goal has its obstacles, but the milestones help us navigate the path. By celebrating our milestones, we squash such beliefs and generate momentum.

To make progress on any musical instrument, we have to understand that music fundamentals are all intertwined. For example, you won't be able to sight-read well if you struggle to read the notes. You won't achieve rhythmical accuracy if you can't play with the aid of a metronome. You'll always struggle to play music *expressively* if you can't play the notes and rhythm confidently. The list goes on, which is why a holistic approach to learning is essential.

Review and Congratulate
Before you begin planning your next steps, the first stage is to *celebrate* your recent achievements. Sadly, this is often something we don't do enough of, particularly as adults. On a day to day basis, we fail to see the progress that we're making. It's a bit like when you're on a diet, and you don't notice the weight loss for yourself. It's only when that friend says, "wow, you're looking good, have you lost a lot of weight?" that you take notice and see yourself in a different light.

Music practice can often be the same. On a day-to-day basis, we don't see how far we've come. It's essential therefore, to reflect on the progress we've made as it builds our confidence and creates momentum. It propels us forward. Perhaps you've recently purchased an instrument so you can fulfil your dream of learning to play. You may have been thinking about learning to play for years, so buying that instrument was a huge step forward in your action plan. If this is you, feel free to congratulate yourself! It could be completing a piece that you've wanted to play, performing in front of people for the first time or practising for several consecutive days.

Any win, big or small, is an achievement that you should celebrate. I love acknowledging people's musical accomplishments, so please share your recent successes in the free Facebook group 'Music Lessons and Practice.'

Task!

Start today by writing down three to five things that you've recently achieved with your music.

Establishing good habits is paramount to the success of achieving our goals. When setting goals, you need to ask yourself exactly what it is you want to achieve.

Here are my suggestions for 16 practice habits that every adult learner should adopt. Remember, good habits support us, while bad habits often make a situation worse. Taking the time to develop these 16 practice habits will help you make progress, which will, in turn, give you the confidence you need to move forward.

It's important to understand that sitting down at your instrument and practising, even if you do that every day, is not enough for you to become a good player. If you want to sound musical and attain proficiency in your playing, there are other things that you have to incorporate regularly into your practice.

16 Practice Habits to Adopt

Following these 16 practice habits will help you achieve more musicality in your playing. They'll also give you the necessary skills to develop the technique and the resilience that playing music requires.

1. Persistence
It's not easy to accomplish anything. Every goal has its obstacles. You are likely to encounter traits such as procrastination and frustration; you'll need a certain amount of willpower to form the habits which drive momentum. The ability to *overcome* such characteristics often separates those who succeed from those who fail. You need to create solutions

in the planning stage to prevent you from relying on willpower alone.

2. Deliberate Practice

When taking action, you need to develop the skill to practice deliberately. Deliberate practice means that your practice sessions include specific tasks that help you fulfil your goals. These tasks should be intentional, appropriate for the level and include methods that will ensure you improve. You will need to break down your practice into achievable bite-sized chunks that allow you to measure progress. You'll also need to listen more so that you can learn, correct and improve.

3. Listening to Music

Listening to music is a great way to make progress, and it's something you can do while completing other tasks. Comparing professional recordings is a fantastic way to learn about musical interpretation and develop your stylistic awareness. You can listen to people on YouTube and consider what makes their performance good or bad. You should also listen to your playing regularly by recording your practice sessions and listening back. It will help you understand what areas need further practice. Here's what Clive, one of my 'Learn Music Together' members, had to say about his first attempt at recording himself:

"It was not easy, and as a reflective practitioner, I found plenty to learn from. Your email's final quotation was particularly appropriate as I looked back on the experience and realised how much this exercise

has helped me. It was, in some ways a catalogue of errors and inexperience on my part. " **Clive**

4. Flexible Approach

Humans are creatures of habit and often do the same thing, but expect the results to change somehow. Learners can be guilty of this in their practise sessions, going through the motions each day and structuring their practice in the same way. Remember the old adage 'If you always do what you always did, then you will always get what you always got.' Clumsy, as it might be, the sentiment is undeniably true. A flexible approach is necessary to make progress. Finding what lies at the root of the problem will then help you create solutions. So if you've been practising a passage for several days and you're not seeing improvements, then it's time to find a different method.

- Can you slow it down?
- Can you practice with different rhythms?
- Have you tried skeleton playing, visualisation, analysing the hand position, checking the fingering etc.? There's more to come on these ideas, so keep on reading.

Whatever you do, don't just keep repeating the methods you've tried already. Be flexible in your practice methods.

5. Mindful Approach

Learners love to play rather than think. Taking a more mindful approach is necessary to improve. It's all too easy in the modern world to get distracted and we are not used to being fully aware of our actions. I'm sure you've experienced going through the motions of practise while your mind is elsewhere. Mistakes happen in the practice room because we are not fully present in the moment. Every action you do should be intentional and in the service of striving for improvement. Being mindful of your posture, any tension in your body, and your tone are things that learners can overlook as their focus tends to be on pitch and rhythm only.

6. Strive for Accuracy

Of course, we should always strive for accuracy within our music practice. Accuracy is, without a doubt, something few would disagree is of upmost importance. However, merely repeating the passage is not an effective way of achieving precision. Sure, it can help, but you need to use a metronome and incorporate other habits such as listening and recording yourself. Whether it's notational, rhythmical, or finger placement precision, you should always strive to improve the musical outcome. Breaking down the sections into bite-sized chunks, practising slowly, recording and listening back are sure ways to make progress.

7. Find Solutions to Problems

To achieve your goals, you've got to be able to find solutions to problems. There are always obstacles that will get in your way and challenges that can lead to frustration. You need to take the time to think about the *cause* of the problem. Often the answer lies much deeper than you think. Sharon, one of my members, came to me for some performance advice. Her piece sounded ok, but she was struggling to elevate it further. We got chatting, and I discovered that her past experiences were preventing her from making progress. It was her opinion that the piece was not good enough to perform as she wasn't playing it *flawlessly*. As I explained to Sharon, professionals don't play flawlessly either they just play their mistakes well. As I dug a little deeper, I learnt that Sharon used to take piano lessons at the convent. The nuns were strict, and they would blame lack of practice for any errors. The fear of making a mistake made Sharon so anxious that she couldn't let go and enjoy the music. She was trying too hard, so I walked her through a few exercises to practice letting go. A week later, Sharon performed her piece, and it was like a different person had taken over.

One of the critical areas of practice for professional players and sportspeople is finding solutions to problems. It's often not easy to overcome difficulties, and finding a good teacher is usually the best way. That said, learning any new skill is challenging. It's not always going to be fun, and progress is rarely fast or easy. If it were, we'd all be accomplished musicians.

Let's say you're someone who struggles to find the time to practice. What solutions can you create to solve this problem? Here are a few suggestions:

• Have you got a list of things you can do without your instrument?

- Can you find the time to do two 10 minute practice sessions a day rather than 20 minute ones? Even a few minutes of practice is better than none.
- Do you have everything prepared and laid out in your practice area so you can get started straight away?

Another common problem that people ask for help with is the ability to play faster. Here are a few suggestions to consider.

- Have you checked your hand position?
- Is your technique strong enough to play at that speed?
- Have you played a wide enough variety of music to accomplish that tempo?
- Can you use a metronome to increase the speed?
- Have you tried practicing the passage with different rhythms?
- Do you know the notes from memory?

Asking yourself such questions is a fantastic way of kick-starting your way to finding and creating solutions.

8. Learn from Past Experiences

You need to develop the ability to learn from the past. We can acquire so much knowledge from our past experiences concerning practice methods, performance stress, and musical weakness, to name but a few. It's also beneficial to regularly revisit music that we've previously studied. Learners are often overly keen to move on to the next challenge, new rhythm, more advanced techniques or new notes. Yet, it is so important to keep developing the fundamentals. A footballer regularly practices goal shooting even when he or she might be the top scorer in the league. A golfer revisits the golf swing basics, and musicians regularly practice fundamentals such as tonal control, articulation balance, and musical awareness. Try incorporating a few minutes to review some repertoire you can play proficiently at the end of every practice session.

9. Communicate Emotion

You need to develop the habit of communicating emotion and conveying the music's expressive nature or characteristics. To do this you've got to be able to play those notes with confidence. So often, learners move on when they can play through a piece reliably and give little thought to the musical intentions that they wish to communicate.

Ask yourself questions regularly when you practise.
- Think about the musical phrases and their contours; ask yourself if you are adding shape, tonal colours and dynamic contrasts.
- Are you breathing at the appropriate time and balancing the melodic line with the accompaniment?
- What is the mood or the character of the piece?
- If it's a dance, are you playing it at a suitable tempo? Does the music tell a story, in which case can the listener recognise the characters?

Listening to recordings is an excellent source of inspiration. It helps to write down your musical intentions and think of ways that you'll communicate them.

10. Use all Your Senses

When you practice, all your senses should be awakened and alert. Your eyes, ears and touch are the most apparent senses related to music. We use our eyes to see the notes, our ears to listen to the sound we are producing, and we rely on touch to play our instruments. However, your sense of smell and taste can also play a role. Some musical styles are evocative of specific countries and flavours and can provide the inspiration you need when composing or performing. Imagine yourself sitting in a tapas bar, being entertained by a Spanish guitarist, or taking yourself to the carnival in Brazil and feeling the samba drums' beat. Using all your senses during your practice sessions will heighten your focus and make you more aware. Don't be afraid of letting your imagination run free, let go and fully submerge yourself in your practice.

11. Be Creative

The habit of being creative is something that you should incorporate into your music practice. It's not enough to sit down and play. We have to tap into our creative side both musically and practically. There are now a plethora of apps that can help you accomplish virtually everything, including planning, recording, looping accompaniments, sight-reading, developing the inner ear, and much more. You can use coloured highlighter tape to help you analyse and prepare your music.

You can write a list of practice methods that you can do away from your instrument. You can find a YouTube channel or a blog to follow. You can challenge yourself in the practice room, by doing silly things and having fun. Have you ever tried playing your piece backwards or whilst standing on one leg? I don't suggest that you do the latter every day, but it is an enjoyable way of developing your levels of awareness and focus.

The more you step away from your comfort zone, the more you will experience growth in crucial areas, such as resilience, confidence, and fulfilment. Being creative in your practice methods will ensure that you keep moving forward to accomplish your goals.

12. Be Passionate

Being passionate is essential because, without passion, there is no enthusiasm. Hence motivation will be hard to cultivate or even find. When you're passionate about something, you care about it, nurture the required skills, and find it much easier to anticipate the rewards in terms of goals. Being passionate will also help when practice isn't going as well as you'd planned. Often we experience frustrations in the practice room; it's the passion that helps us find the determination to keep going. Without it, it would be all too easy to give up.

It's important to remind ourselves why we're trying to achieve our music goals.

- How will it improve your life?
- How will it improve your playing?
- What will it bring to your musical skills?
- Will it develop a particular aspect of your technique?

The why is the driving force behind the goal and when things get tough, it's a great place to find that bit of extra motivation.

13. Go Beyond Your Comfort Zone

There's a fine line between going beyond your comfort zone and setting ambitious goals that are beyond your reach. However, many of us don't enjoy stepping beyond our comfort zone initially. That said, there's not much satisfaction if we stay with what we already know. Those who do push themselves will tell you that you rarely regret the experience.

My own musical journey might seem like a dream. However, I want you to know that the road has not been without its challenges. Here is a brief account:

I almost packed away my instrument for good a few years ago I was heading to London to take my final exam to become an examiner for Trinity College London. The fear of failing was so immense that I literally stepped off the train at Euston and immediately boarded the train back to Manchester. I felt an unprecedented wave of pressure wash over me. I had trained for six months, and tomorrow I would have a senior examiner watch over me like a hawk. Every word I said to the candidate every comment I wrote and every note I played on the piano would be scrutinised. There is no second chance at every point in the training; fail, and you are out. You have to wait years to reapply. So you can probably understand why the pressure was so much I bailed and hopped back on the train. BUT as I thought about everything I'd invested and evaluated everything I'd learned, I knew I had nothing to lose and everything to gain.

My final assessment went like clockwork, and I thoroughly enjoyed the experience. To top it off, the examination centre was at the Fazioli studios in London. Yes, the exam piano was a Fazioli. I also got a tour around the studios, and the opportunity to a play on a diamond-embellished piano worth over 7 figures, one of the many perks I've experienced in my job. That weekend trip to London changed my life, and I've never looked back.

As an examiner, I'm often asked if I have any tips to overcome nerves in examinations and lessons? The simple answer is you have to practice being in that situation. Being able to play the music in the practice room doesn't mean that you can perform it under pressure or in another location. Far too often, people rely on muscle memory to get them through, and it's not enough. You have to know the music intimately. Performing regularly is essential to conquering those performance anxieties. Put the wheels in motion by setting yourself a date for your next performance and share it with someone.

One of the most challenging decisions I had to make in writing this book was when to tell others. My close friends have been aware that I've been writing for years, but that wasn't enough to help this book get to the finishing line. I had to step outside my comfort zone and put my intentions out there, which I did by telling my email community. Here's a snippet of what I wrote:

"Having created an overview of the book, it is time to hold myself accountable. I can't tell you how hard it was to put it out there to the world on Tuesday. I put that email back into draft twice. However, I'm no stranger to taking a walk on the wild side, and I know that you make the greatest strides forwards when you step outside your comfort zone."

There is, however, a delicate balance between ambition and reality. While you can learn to play any piece if you are prepared to practice for long enough, it's unlikely that you'll experience much joy in the process. Not to mention the knowledge you gain is often not transferrable. There's no point setting yourself up to fail. Many people in this world take graded music examinations, but that doesn't necessarily mean they are competent players. Often their repertoire is limited to the examination pieces which they spent months learning. To really enjoy your playing now and in the future, you need to build musical foundations that will last. Think of a building, without solid foundations, no matter how much you invest in the interior, cracks will appear. Further down the line, those cracks are expensive to fix which is why architects invest so much in the groundwork.

14. Enjoy Playing

While playing new pieces is an integral part of practice, it is equally crucial to have fun playing. As I mentioned previously, too often, learners focus only on new things. They forget that there's lots of pleasure to be had in playing music that you enjoy and are already familiar with. When choosing repertoire to perform, always start with something you feel confident at playing. It's good practice to end your sessions by playing pieces that you already know. Enjoyment is part of the learning process, and without it, motivation and enthusiasm are hard to kindle.

15. Play With Others

Playing with other people is a fantastic way to learn, particularly if you play with someone who's at a higher level than yourself. Participating in ensembles and duets strengthens your sight-reading skills, your aural awareness and your ability to play on through mistakes. They're a great way of taking your playing to another level. That's why every month inside of the 'Learn Music Together Academy', there's an ensemble piece. Members practice with the accompaniment, and then the parts are put together in a video. Not only does it help members make progress musically, the finished video gives them an opportunity to share the success of their achievements with others. It boosts their confidence, and brings joy to others when they share the music. It's a win, win all round.

16. Never Stop Learning

Remember, you're never too old to learn. There are always new skills and techniques for us to adopt. Self-growth is one of the key elements to living a fulfilling life and our brains have the capacity to keep learning at any age. Acquiring new skills is a great way to keep the mind sharp and fill you with happiness. While the learning process can be challenging and sometimes push you to the limits, it's an incredible feeling when you achieve your goals. When you play something you never thought possible, pass an exam, perform your first solo or share your playing with others, it creates a sense of personal achievement that makes us happier. It gives added purpose to our lives and enhances our enjoyment, which is why it's so important to celebrate those accomplishments with pride.

How to Plan Your Music Goals.

To learn anything, you've got to be fully focused and engaged. To accomplish any goal, you need to believe that you're up to the challenge; learning an instrument isn't easy. When you formulate goals, you need to make sure that they are specific and measurable. Our experiences are influenced by our expectations and as we get older, self-doubt, unfortunately, becomes more and more of an enemy. You have to believe in yourself and that you are capable of rising to the challenge. When setting these goals, make sure you are in a positive mindset and abolish any thoughts of doubt. It's also important to realise why achieving them matters to you. What is it going to help you master? Or how is it going to make you feel? The *why* becomes beneficial when we're struggling to achieve goals, and, of course, inevitably, there will be struggles. Anything that you want to accomplish always has its road blocks. It's at times like these that we fall back on our habits. **Remember: Good habits get us through those obstacles.**

No challenge is ever easy; it would be delusional to think so. Establishing good habits often requires determination. When planning goals, you need to incorporate a little of all 16 practice habits. Applying the acronym SMART, is an excellent way to formulate your musical goals.

Specific   Measurable   Achievable   Rewarding   Time frame

The SMART system will ensure that your goals are clear, achievable and quantifiable. You need to have absolute clarity on what you want to accomplish and why the goal is important to you.

How to Make a Goal Specific.
Say your goal is, for example, *'I want to practice more.'* Just stating *'I want to practice more'* is not a well-formulated goal because it's not specific, nor is it measurable. Always remember that poorly formulated goals are goals easily forgotten.

Let's look at how we could change that statement into a more specific and measurable goal.

Instead of saying, 'I want to practice more,' ask yourself: How many times in the week do you want to practice and when?

So let's say I'm going to practice five times a week before breakfast.

Now let's make that goal more measurable by asking how long are you going to practice for?

I'm going to practice five times a week for 20 minutes each practice session, before breakfast.

The next step is to ascertain whether your goal is achievable. For example, if I'd have said that I'm going to practice three times a day for 20 minutes *every* day of the week, when currently, I do very little practice, then that goal is probably not going to be achievable.

Ask yourself if you can accomplish the goals you set. Remember, you want to push yourself a little, but the goals still need to be realistic. We want to set ourselves up for success, not failure.

The next step is to ensure your musical goal is rewarding. Hopefully, as practice is an essential part of making progress, the reward will be simply experiencing that you're getting better. However, rewards could take other forms, so be creative.

Finally, you want to set a timeframe. So how long are you going to measure your routine to see if you're successful? The best way to do this is to add a deadline, for example, March 31st.

My Practice Goal now has time parameters and is much more measurable and specific:

'I will practice five times a week for 20 minutes in the morning before breakfast between now and March 31st.'

Let's take another example.
Say you want to play more pieces. Again this is very generalised. Let's be specific. How many pieces of repertoire do you want to learn, and whatis the timeframe you will give yourself? My advice to students is: *'aim to learn one new piece per week.'* If it takes several weeks, then you should be asking yourself why? Do you need to take a step back and improve your sight-reading or technique, for example?

Let's say I want to learn 12 new pieces over three months.

Be more specific and decide which particular styles of music you want to learn, such as I will learn 12 *new pieces* in *four* different styles over the next 3 *months.* That's measurable and specific because you can tick those pieces off as you accomplish them. You can say, yes, I achieved that goal, or no, I didn't achieve that goal.

It can be hard to know where to begin when setting music goals. The most important thing is a regular practice regime.

So make sure if you don't already have a goal for practice sessions, you start there.

You'll find traits such as motivation, confidence, and resilience, undulate like waves in the ocean. On a calm day, things will seem swimmingly easy, but there will be storms that could throw you off course. Hence, evaluating your actions and making sure they're rewarding is essential. It also helps to put a contingency plan in place to help when things get challenging. It's beneficial to regularly ask yourself if the action you are doing or the thought you are feeling is helping you move forward in achieving goals.

Once you've considered your goals you'll want to incorporate the 16 practice habits. This will ensure that you're not just going tunnel-visioned down one path. Music is a complex subject, and there are lots of elements, which are intertwined. For example, to get better at sight-reading, you need good pattern recognition. You also need to be confident at reading notation and rhythm. Let's say you want to improve your improvisation skills, in which case, you'll need to know about chord structure and have a good sense of rhythm.

In addition, you'll also need an understanding of chord symbols, and good listening skills. To improve your practice skills, you need to focus on notation, rhythm, speed, theory, aural, composition, communication etc. All the different elements in music connect.

You should strive to take a holistic approach as you need to understand how one thing supports another. Taking an all-encompassing approach will help you grow in a more musical way.

Task!

Map out some musical goals using the SMART formula. Then select **three to five goals to focus on.** Three is probably enough for each quarter of the year.

Create Actionable Steps
The goal is like the final destination, but to get there, you will need to create actionable steps to ensure you keep moving forwards.

Here are a few examples of goals you might set and the stepping stones you could create to achieve those goals.

Say your goal is to choose three pieces this month, so you can develop your communications skills and musical awareness.

STEP 1
- Choose one piece that has a wide range of dynamics.

STEP 2
- Choose a piece in a dance style, such as a waltz.

STEP 3
- Find a lively piece with a mix of articulation patterns.

STEP 4
- Create a playlist on YouTube of the pieces that you are going to learn.

STEP 5
- Find online resources to support learning more about communication skills and musical awareness.

STEP 6
- Find different ways to measure progress. Keep a log of metronome marks and record yourself playing long notes at different dynamic levels each week. You could use a decibel meter app to track your contrasts.

Here's another example.

Let's say your goal is to practice five times a week for 20 minutes. Ask yourself what you can do to help you take action towards accomplishing this goal?

STEP 1
- Set a reminder on your phone every day to signal when it's time to practice.

STEP 2
- Write a practice plan each Sunday that includes what you will do in every practice session.

STEP 3
- Mark your practice on the family calendar and create a 'do not disturb sign' for the door.

STEP 4
- Find a suitable quote and attach it to your piano or music stand to remind you why you want to practice.

STEP 5
- Make a practice calendar, get a practice notebook and make sure that there's a pencil pot by your instrument.

STEP 6
- Reflect on your achievements at the end of every practice so that you can look back and see how much progress you've made each month.

Sometimes when we practise, it's not just about us. We have to fit that in with our families and their needs. Set the boundaries and tell those at home not to disturb you during these times as you will be practising.

By breaking down the steps, it makes it easier to make progress towards the finishing line. Each of those little steps feels like you're taking action and helps you gain momentum towards accomplishing your goals. Music is a passion, and likemany others, it is a never-ending journey. There are always new things to learn, explore and enjoy. Regularly setting aims, objectives, and goals is beneficial in keeping you on a path that ensures you are improving and not meandering.

Commit to Your Musical Goals.
Studies have shown that when you write down your goals, share them, and show others your intentions, the likelihood of success increases by as much as two to three times. I regularly ask what your goals are for the month on my Facebook page **Musician in the Making,** and I would love you to share yours in the comments.

Setting habits and attaining goals is not easy. Anything worth doing has its challenges. Finding yourself an *accountability partner* and surrounding yourself with like-minded people is crucial. It's the ability to push through those challenges *with the right support* that often separates those who succeed from those who fail. Having an accountability partner, someone who checks that you are sticking to your plan, is a fantastic way of gaining the support that you need.

Bev, Anne and Dolores are three members of Learn Music Together who meet regularly in an accountability group. Not only have they formed a friendship across the world. (Bev lives in Canada, Dolores in England and Anne in Dublin), but they have supported one another and made progress together along their musical journeys. Recently they have been encouraging one another daily by sending a 'thumbs up' message every time they practice. Dolores told me that it gave her a great feeling of responsibility, and it has helped her establish a daily routine. She'll be the first to admit that she finds it challenging to maintain a regular practice regime, so receiving a text each day from her 'accountability buddies' motivates her to take action. Anne said that without the group, she would have given up long ago. The method of giving each other a daily boost is so rewarding. We all benefit, and it's fantastic knowing that we are inspiring one another.

Ultimately, when we set goals, it should be about the journey and not the destination. You want to make sure that you form habits and put things in place to help you move forward. At the University of London, studies have shown that it's tough to develop habits. On average, it takes 66 days to make a habit into something you no longer have to consciously think about. At the far end of the spectrum, it can take as long as 250 days, so be prepared. Change does not happen instantly. Habits are formulated over a long period of time, and there will always be difficulties along the way. You need to have a way of overcoming those obstacles to help you navigate the path when times get tough. Another way that you can gain support is by being actively involved in a community. There are lots of Facebook groups and associations that you could join. The community inside the Learn Music Together Academy is a fantastic place to get support.

Achieving your goals is a sure way of ensuring you stay committed, make progress and enjoy learning to play your instruments. Remember, you can always change your goals as you progress, and it's always advisory to undergo an annual review of them and your successes. You may not achieve all your goals on your first attempt, but don't let this deter you. Here's a top tip from Avril who is a member of my LMT community.

'FAIL stands for first attempt in learning. You may not always get it right, but you'll never move forward if you don't get started in the first place.'

Section 3

Practice Methods

Chapter 6 - Practice Diary

It's common to take a list to the supermarket or grocery store so you don't forget any of those essential items. However, less than 20% of people write down their goals or keep a detailed practice diary. I don't mean a book that your teacher writes about what you are supposed to practice; I'm talking about a journal documenting your daily progress. Learners who plan out their practice sessions are up to one and half times more likely to accomplish their tasks. However, it gets even better; those who review what they've written 24 hours later can increase their memory retention by up to 70 %. Let's just think about that for a moment. When practising, say you keep getting the fingering wrong on beat 2 of bar 3. Take the time to put a note in your practice diary.

'In bar 3 on beat two, I keep playing the F with finger 3, and it needs to be finger 2. I need to work at stretching my second finger out and think about that action earlier.'

By writing that down, you are 1.5 times more likely to think about that in your next practice session. Better still, your awareness will increase up to 70% if you read that note to yourself before practising that bar again the following day. Many learners think it takes too much time to keep a detailed practice diary. They'd rather spend the time repeating the action physically, as they believe they will get a quicker result. However, neurologists will tell you differently.

A practice diary gives you an external resource which you can refer to and follow. Plus, by writing things down, you are helping your brain form a memory. When you put pen to paper, a deeper action takes place called encoding. Encoding is a process which puts information into our memory in a way that makes it accessible. Things that we perceive and analyse move to our long-term memory when we write them down. Hence you increase your chances of remembering them.

There are numerous other benefits to keeping a practice diary, so let's look at some of them.

1. Planning allows you to make the most of your time

When you plan ahead, it prevents that feeling of being overwhelmed and helps you keep a clear mind. You can see quickly what to prioritise and therefore take action straight away.

2. Enables a higher level of thinking

Reviewing and planning your practice sessions involves a lot of higher order thinking, which helps you consolidate your goals and level of progress. When you write things down, you're more likely to process your actions, discover opportunities for improvement and see the results of your efforts. Based on this, you can take more focused action in the future.

3. Encourages daily progress

Evaluating your past and current practice sessions allows you to gauge your strengths and weaknesses. You can measure your progress which can be rewarding. On the other hand, you are more likely to spot what isn't working and change your method. Keeping a practice diary is a fantastic way of processing your emotions on a much deeper level.

4. Keeps you motivated

Practising can be frustrating, and you'll undoubtedly have peaks and troughs in your levels of success. When the chips are down, looking through your practice diary can help you realise how far you've come and where there are opportunities to make improvements.

5. Record of the past

We would all like to think that we can remember things, but the reality is that even our biggest achievements can get lost in our minds. A practice diary is an invaluable insight into your musical journey. Reading through your achievements can often enhance your level of self-trust and belief.

6. Makes you more committed

Habits are hard to break, and if you establish a habit of writing in your practice diary, you are more likely to keep to your routine. There's nothing more rewarding than ticking off your daily to-do list.

7. Develops a deeper level of gratitude

We often forget how much we have to celebrate; sadly, far too many of us wallow in our failures. I know from experience that if 98 people congratulate me for a performance and 2 criticise me, I am far more likely to remember those negative responses. I've learnt a lot about myself through my musical journey. I used to dwell for days on those negative comments. They ate away at me and took away any joy that I had experienced. While criticism can be a useful resource for learning going forward, sometimes you just have to accept that it is impossible to please everyone. It's often the case that those who only criticise do so because they are jealous of your achievements. If anyone has ever made a joke about you learning to play an instrument, they've probably done so out of envy rather than mockery. After any performance, write down some of those positive comments. They'll serve as a great reminder of how far you've come not only now but into the future.

Did you know that Oprah Winfrey keeps a gratitude diary? She claims that it helps her stay grounded and grateful for her achievements. It doesn't matter how famous you become; those negative thoughts are hard to eliminate. So while they can be helpful, they can also be detrimental. By writing down the positives, we form a deeper connection with our learning. It helps us be more mindful of our musical achievements.

What type of diary should you buy?
While there are many practice diaries that you can purchase, a simple exercise book is all you need. I like to keep a list of music that I want to learn at the back and often jot down pieces that I've enjoyed listening to. I then take a page for each day and plan my sessions ahead of schedule, usually in one-week

blocks. Although if I am preparing for a recital, I will make a longer-term plan. When I start a new piece of music, I study the score and then divide it into bite-sized sections. Each one of these sections is then allocated a slot in my plan.

I write down what I will do in my warm-up and which section of the piece I will focus on during the session. I make notes on things that I will find challenging within the music, what I will need to be aware of, such as articulation patterns, dynamics, and intonation challenges. I also note any metronome speeds and musical thoughts. At the end of my session, I'll write down what I achieved, what went well, what needs further work and why. If I note that something didn't go well, I'll look into why and how I might use an alternative method in my next session.

To help you get started, planning your diary here are a few tips:

Plan a clear focus for each session.
Nothing kills progress, like trying to do everything.
If you're trying to get everything correct at once, for example, playing the notes with the correct rhythm, articulation, dynamics and hoping it will sound musical, then you've set an impossible task for yourself. Whatever level you are at, trying to accomplish everything without a clear plan is too much. So work on one thing at a time in your practice session. Choose only a few bars and focus on making them fantastic. Clap out the rhythm before you play it; think about the notes. Put the

notes and the rhythm together slowly. Then think about the tone, balance and shape.

Think about problems

So often adult learners, repeat things endlessly in the hope that they will make progress. However, all that happens is you strengthen the errors. Instead, ask yourself what's causing the problem.

- Could it be that you are playing the rhythm incorrectly?
- Maybe you are not using the best fingering.
- Perhaps you are finding the coordination difficult?
- Or your left hand is playing too loud for the expressive melody to sound musical.

Once you know the problem, you can create a solution.

Reflect on Your Progress

Reflecting upon your achievements and assessing which bars need further work is an essential part of practice. It helps you map out your progress and see where your strengths and weaknesses are. In your next practice session, you can then build on these. If something didn't work yesterday, you need to change your approach. It's unlikely to improve if you do the same thing, so get creative with your methods, perhaps do a bit of research, or seek out some advice.

You can download a template for your practice diary at https://playmusicbetterbook.com/resources

Of course, you can 'go more to town' on documenting your progress. For one of my 'Learn Music Together' members, Dennis, his practice diary turned into a blog. He talks about *falling off the practice wagon* and how he uses my methods *to get the wheels turning again.* What I love about Dennis's blog is his passion and willingness to share with raw honesty. For every piece he learns, he creates a video that tells a story. Nothing elaborate, but it's enough that people connect and resonate with him. Other members love listening to him play. His music is not perfect; he'll be the first to say that he still has a lot to learn. But it's the honesty and his commitment that makes these performances so appealing. Dennis is a true inspiration to any adult learning to play.

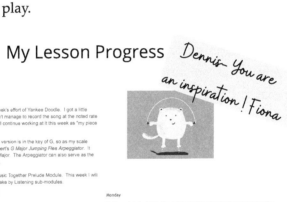

My Lesson Progress

Dennis~ You are an inspiration! Fiona

Prelude · Week 3

Thanks to everyone who complemented last week's effort of Yankee Doodle. I got a little carried away with producing the video, and didn't manage to record the song at the noted rate of 120 bpm, but could only manage 100bpm. I'll continue working at it this week as "my piece to enjoy".

The song for this week is Amazing Grace. This version is in the key of G, so as my scale practice warm up routine I will use the Gary Jugert's *G Major Jumping Flea Arpeggiator.* It covers the notes and chord progressions of G Major. The Arpeggiator can also serve as the object of sight reading and metronome practice.

I will continue on with the topics in the Learn Music Together Prelude Module. This week I will focus on the Sight Reading and Spotting a Mistake by Listening sub-modules.

Monday, May 31, 2021

Restart

I seem to have fallen off the wagon lately, so I'm going to try a restart.

I'm still working on Home on the Range, but progress is slow.

Today (May31, 2021), I am listening to Fiona's Sight Reading With Confidence, Part 1. I'll continue on with the other parts each day as appropriate.

- Fiona said we should learn one new piece each week. I can usually get the notes, but not at the indicated tempo
- I like the "words" to play. I need to improve on location of notes on the fretboard.

June 1 · Watched Fiona's Sight Reading With Confidence, Part 1. I need to practice sight reading by

- find a sight reading app
- read through names of notes on my music

Monday

Starting again today. Watched Fiona's first video in the Prelude section, *Prelude Overview*

Watched Fiona's *What Practice Means* Intro. Didn't go any further 'cause Fiona said to watch only one video per day.

I recently started a new course, *Ukulele Fingerstyle Basics.* I will apply Fiona's instructions to that course.

6. All Through the Night

Chapter 7 - Posture

As a child, I remember frequently being told to sit up, especially in school assemblies. Mrs Hayward would stand at the front of the hall and say things like, 'Do you want to look like old Mother Hubbard when you grow up? Please stop slouching and uncross your legs. If you don't, you'll get varicose veins when you're older.' I often wonder why she referred to 'Old Mother Hubbard', however, if you search Google Images, she's nearly always depicted as an old lady bent over.

We all know that good posture is essential for playing an instrument, but how much do you think about it when you play? Probably not much at all, after the initial few bars. Yet posture has so much to do with the success of our music making. Playing a musical instrument involves many different muscles in your body, and your posture impacts every single note you play. Regardless of what instrument you are trying to master, always consider your body to be an extension of your instrument. You are one together, and every part of your body affects the sound you produce. The tone quality, the projection of sound, the ability to coordinate and digest information, are all examples of things which can be negatively affected by bad posture.

No matter what instrument you play, your head, your back, your eyes, your shoulders, even your balance, and breathing need consideration. All of these things can compromise the musical outcome.

As you get older you are more likely to have some bad habits in your posture. By habit, I mean a pattern of behaviour which you have developed in the past and now repeat automatically. Slouching is a perfect example. These habits affect how our bodies function, and it's surprising the number of people who are unaware that they are compromising their ability to play.

Our posture is also affected by our mindset. Our bodies react differently in certain situations. For example, if you're nervous, you might get sweaty palms, or suffer from shaky hands. When you are frustrated, your shoulders will most likely become tense. Habits are familiar, and we find them reassuring whether they are *good* or *bad*. Unfortunately, habits usually take place in our subconscious so we do things automatically, which is why they're difficult to change.

There is a close relationship between learning new skills and our habits. Whenever you start a new skill, you develop patterns of behaviour. Initially, you do your best to get things right. For example, when you first started learning to play your instrument, you would have been more mindful of your hand position or how you stand. However, over time, if we're not careful, we pay less and less attention to how we hold an instrument because our habits become automatic responses. We become inflexible in the way we do things and can be reluctant to change or find it challenging to adapt. Often change causes us to regress for a while, but a period of consolidation can help us to make greater strides forward. This isn't a bad thing, but it can feel that way. It's like tidying a cupboard that's overflowing with things; we've all got a place like that. It's the home for all items that don't have a place. It's the door you dread opening as you know things will immediately fall out. To tidy the cupboard, you first have to empty it, which initially creates even more mess. Surrounded by a pile, you sort through the clutter, dispose of unwanted items and place the rest of the things back in a tidy fashion. It takes several hours, but the finished result is so rewarding. The door now closes properly, and there's almost an emptiness about the cupboard. Things now feel like they have a place and there's space for new additions. Ultimately, it can be very reassuring.

When changing things with your posture, it will likely make things worse before it improves. Change makes us feel uncomfortable because it means breaking a habit. However, that doesn't mean it's wrong. It takes time for changes to make an impact and often lots of patience and perseverance.

The problem with many adults is they like instant results. They judge themselves by the outcome as opposed to evaluating the process and seeing what they've learnt along the way. Think of a child learning to walk. They have no preconceptions, and place no pressure upon themselves to accomplish the skill. They don't look at the end result, nor do they judge or compare themselves.

A toddler never thinks, 'Oh I should be able to do this by now.' They don't see other children at playgroup and think they can walk, so I should be able to. It's only the grown-ups around them that set the expectations.

Think back to the amazing determination and resilience you once had as a toddler learning to walk. You were happy to just keep trying until you succeeded. I say think back, but that's the problem, we can't remember the days when learning difficult skills was fun and a game. When things go wrong in the adult world, we rarely laugh and remain happy; negative thoughts take over instead. While we're on the subject of negative thoughts, if you are reading this and think you can't teach an old dog new tricks, think again.

It doesn't matter how old you are. If you want to learn and improve, you can form new habits. Professional sportspeople of all ages have an entourage of people who help them change their habits to achieve their goals. Physiotherapists, psychologists, dieticians and coaches continuously help them improve the development of their minds and body by reviewing their practices and making small changes. It isn't easy by yourself, but it is totally doable. The human brain is an amazing organ. The latest studies in neurology now show that your brain has the capacity to keep learning and mastering skills no matter how old you are. Sure the process may not be as easy as in your younger days, but don't let that stop you.

To make change, you've got to review your habits and recommit to them regularly. By improving your posture and raising your awareness, you will get better results from your practice sessions. However, you can't fix everything at once. To get started, choose one or two things to focus on and keep returning to this chapter to learn more.

I want you to remember to be kind to yourself. Negative habits are often a result of trying too hard or being too fixated on the end result. For learners, it's always about how many pieces can you play? How fast can you play? How accurately can you play? These are all examples of an end result. You'll find that progress happens by itself if you study the process and develop sustainable habits.

> **Focus on the now. Be aware and adapt throughout the learning process rather than judging things by the end result.**

Finally, you need to be aware that to change your posture you'll need to implement those changes in your daily life. You can't have one posture to play an instrument and another posture for your everyday life. You've got to think about these things 24 seven.

There's an easy but highly effective tip that I'd love to share with you to get you started.

Keep Your Head Up and Forward.

Whatever level you are at and whatever instrument you play, keeping your head up and forwards will improve everything. So often, I see learners leaning forwards towards their instrument, especially when sight-reading.

In doing this, you compromise your breathing and create tension in the body. Both of these things make it harder to move freely and control your instrument. Keeping the head balanced and in its right place is the first thing to be mindful of when practising. As we get older, we tend to bow our heads more.

Why is the head in relation to the spine so important?
The head and the spine influence the whole body. So if your head is slightly out of line, it compromises the way our bodies move.

Try for a moment lowering your head and then raising your arm. Notice how the weight and tension in your arm, shoulder and neck feel. Now align your head forwards and slightly up and raise your arm. Do you notice any difference in the tension and how the muscles feel?

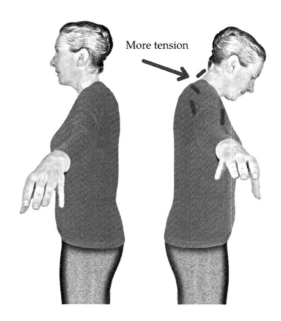

More tension

If your head is too far forward, it compromises your ability to breathe. Similarly, if your head is back, your ability to breathe is impacted. If you twist to one side, this compromises your ability to both breathe *and* move.

When your head is balanced, it feels much lighter. Experiment a little and think about how the tension feels in your neck. If you tip your head forwards, you'll feel the back of your neck pull. And if you tip it backwards, you'll feel your voice and your throat strain. Slowly bring it back to the middle and then just move it forward and up slightly. Eventually you should find that perfect balancing point and when you get there, you'll sense the freedom at the back of your neck, and your head will feel lighter.

The next time you practice, be aware of your head position. If you play the piano, ask yourself if you are looking down at the keys far more than you should. If you play a wind or brass instrument, do you lower your head to play? A common problem for saxophonists is having their neck straps too low, which means the head has to lower in order to blow into the mouthpiece. If you are a string player, do you look at the strings or the fretboard when you play?

Almost every adult who plays an instrument is guilty of putting their head too far forward or leaning it to one side, if they are not mindful of their posture.

As of today, I would love you to make a promise to yourself that you are going to change this habit. Those who do will notice a huge difference in their tone. It will also make you feel more confident and allow you to move and co-ordinate with much more ease.

The Jaw

When we concentrate, it's common to hold tension in the jaw, without being aware that we are doing so. If you grit your teeth for a moment, you'll be able to feel that your throat and the muscles behind your ears tighten. A similar thing occurs when you press your tongue to the roof of the mouth.

Holding tension in the jaw restricts your breathing and often happens when sight-reading or playing music which you find challenging.

If you know that you tend to tighten the jaw, try speaking aloud when you practice that passage. Or if that's not possible because you play a wind instrument, imagine you are talking aloud. You'll hear that the projection of sound is much greater if your jaw is relaxed.

Your Eyes

Whether you read music or play by ear, how you focus your eyes will affect the sound you produce. It's not uncommon when practising to over-focus, especially if you are unfamiliar with the music. Have you ever had that experience of losing where you are on the page? That's usually a result of over-focusing.

If you play by ear, there's often a tendency to fixate the eyes on a part of your instrument or on a fixed spot in the room. When you stare at something for any length of time, your eyes tighten, which compromises your visual system. This, in turn, affects your head and your coordination. Straining the eyes also reduces the amount of information that your brain can digest. If you are one of those people who leans forward and stares at the music, particularly when sight- reading, you're actually hindering yourself significantly. You are restricting the amount of information that the brain can digest.

One of the best things you can do to prevent over-focusing is toanalyse your music. Using highlighters to raise awareness of certain aspects within the piece will help. If you haven't read the earlier chapter 3 'A Quick win' turn back and do so now.

Another great way to prevent overstraining the eyes is to ask yourself questions. Before you play, take a look at the music fora few seconds, then close your eyes and see what you can recall.

- Can you remember the time signature?
- Can you recall the first notes of the piece?
- Can you clap the rhythm?

Now don't compete with yourself here. There's no right amount to remember. Repeat the exercise several times; you'll be surprised at how much information you can absorb.

When you play, you should try to keep a panoramic vision. Try and read ahead in the music and be aware of your surroundings, not just the music or a part of your instrument. If you play by ear, make sure that you're taking in more of a peripheral view. Make things easier for yourself by ensuring your practice space has good lighting. Don't just use as Peter Kay, the comedian, calls it so amusingly, 'the big light in the room' in your practice space. Have an extra lamp by your piano or music stand as it will improve your quality of vision.

Make sure you adjust the music stand so that it's at the appropriate height. It always makes me laugh how many people blame the music stand for not seeing the music properly. Cheap music stands can be flimsy, especially when you try and make them higher. Often they don't go high enough, so if necessary, put your stand on a small table, or stand further back.

If you sit to play your instrument, consider adjusting the piano stool or chair to make it a bit higher or lower so that the music is easier to see. We invest so much in our instruments, but we often neglect the accessories that will make our practise sessions so much more enjoyable and productive.

Body Mapping

To play any instrument well, your body has to move freely and coordinate with ease. Understanding how the body works can help you gain more freedom of movement. The muscles throughout our bodies are all connected, and the way we breathe affects muscle movements. Wind and brass players tend to be more mindful of this, but breathing has an important role for anyone learning to play an instrument.

The body's primary function is to breathe; let's face it, if it weren't, none of us would be here. When you restrict the respiratory system through bad posture, you compromise your ease of coordination.

Whether you stand or sit to play, your feet and legs have a big effect on your breathing. Your breathing also affects your emotional state.

A long muscle called the Psoas muscle connects our diaphragm to the top of our legs, just below the pelvis. If you have any tension in the legs, it will also cause tension in this muscle, which then has an impact on the diaphragm muscles. Hence the way you hold your legs and the way you balance on your feet affects your breathing.

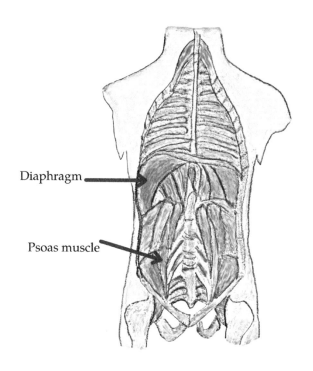

Diaphragm

Psoas muscle

When your breathing is compromised, it impacts the freedom in your shoulders, which in turn affects the freedom in your arms, and impacts the dexterity of your fingers.

Throughout our daily lives, we breathe naturally from the diaphragm. Yet, as soon as somebody tells us to take bigger breaths we tend do the opposite of what we're supposed to. I don't know why this happens, but it happens with most people. When asked to take a big breath, many people breathe from the chest. You'll know if you're doing this because your shoulders will rise up as well as your chest. The easiest way to raise your awareness of breathing from the diaphragm is to lie on the floor. When lying down, you can feel your abdomen rising and lowering. Try placing a book on your abdomen and watch it rise and fall as you breathe in and out.

To gain more awareness of your breathing, breathe in through your nose as you are more likely to breathe from your diaphragm. You need to fill your abdomen as you breathe in. When you do so, you'll notice that there is movement in your lower back too. When you breathe in, you want the back to widen, and as you breathe out, it will narrow again. Any tension in the body restricts this movement.

Here's another exercise to try which will help you to understand the difference. Lock your knees and scrunch up your toes, then lean forward a bit with your head lowered. Now, breathe in from the diaphragm and you'll feel much more restricted. You'll feel the tension in your legs, but you'll also notice that you can't breathe deeply. Your breathing will be much more shallow.

When you practice something tricky on your instrument, you are likely to be more tense, as your level of focus is higher. Often we lean towards the music stand, which constricts the rib cage and both the diaphragm and breathing are compromised. It also restricts your movement, so be aware of your posture when practicing challenging passagework. Stop for a moment and ask yourself, am I leaning in? Am I leaning forwards? Am I tensing my knees? Am I clenching my toes? Take a moment just to anchor your feet back on the floor and relax the knees.

Let's just quickly recap things that compromise your breathing. If you bend your head forwards, backwards, or tense any part of your body including your toes, you'll notice that it's harder to breathe. Be aware of lifting the chest and avoid leaning towards your instrument. Try not to lean in any direction. Keep your head aligned with the spine, and consciously maintain that position.

Try breathing through your nose during the day. It will help you become much more efficient at taking in the air because we use the diaphragm when we breathe through our noses. It's also better for you as you'll get fewer throat infections if you breathe through your nose. Your nose has a filtration system which naturally protects you. If you can adopt the habit of breathing through your nose in your daily life, your breath will flow more freely, and you'll feel much more confident. Taking some deep breaths in through the nose is a great way to lift your spirits and re-energise yourself.

Remember to keep the neck muscles relaxed, and make sure you relax the tension in your spine and abdominal muscles. Relax the throat- talking while you're doing something is a great way to keep the back of the throat relaxed and make sure you're balanced and comfortable.

Here's one final fun exercise to try which will help you raise awareness of breathing in relation to posture. Try reading aloud a paragraph from this book with your legs, buttocks and feet tightly clenched together and see how your voice changes.

It will probably go higher. Then release all that tension and carry on speaking. You'll see that the voice projects and resonates much more. Even if you just have your toes scrunched in your shoes while you're practising, it will have a major impact on the sound that you produce.

Relaxation

Did you know that you are, on average, one centimetre taller in the morning? Throughout the day, the weight of our bodies causes the cartilage in our knees and spine to slowly compress so we shrink. It relaxes again as we sleep. You can learn to expand your body and improve your breathing by practising yoga, tai chi, or pilates. Professional musicians often have an exercise routine that they work through to help them relax and deepen their focus. The one I've outlined below is taken from the Alexander Technique, a method I studied while recovering from tendonitis. It's called the semi-supine position, and it's a great position to adopt when taking a short break during your practice sessions. It will help you relieve any tension, allow your body to relax and extend your breathing. Lying in this position provides a great opportunity to think about what you've been practising and to assess areas to improve. I would encourage everyone to try it for a few minutes at least once daily.

Semi-Supine Position

Ideally, you want to do this exercise on a hard surface such as your floor. However, if it's too challenging to get down there, you could use your bed. Just be aware that modern mattresses are designed to curve to your body, and we are trying to straighten out the back through this exercise.

You will also need a book and possibly a large cushion if you've got any tension in your lower back. You'll need to experiment with the size of the book to find one that keeps your head in line with your spine.

Lie down on the floor with your knees bent. If you've got tension in your lower back, put a cushion on the floor, underneath your feet, as this will provide support and help you relax.

Place a book under your head so that it is in line with your spine. Without a book to support your head, your back will likely arch slightly, and your chin will point more towards the ceiling. You'll know when you have the correct size book as your head will feel lighter.

The picture below illustrates the position you need to adopt.

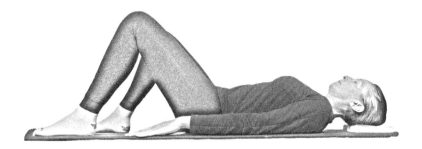

Spend a few moments thinking about your body and how you are feeling. Don't worry about anything else. Think about how your back feels, how your shoulders and neck feel, ask yourself if your knees are locked. If you're struggling to feel comfortable, you may want to put some cushions in various places. You can elevate your feet further by placing a cushion beneath them. Place cushions below your elbows or hands. Make yourself comfortable. Once you feel relaxed start to notice your breathing and see if you can stretch your toes out to find the balancing points in the feet. Relax the jaw and the tongue down. Relax the eyes and release any tension in the neck. Try and open the shoulders out. This is why it's great to do this exercise on a hard floor. You want to try and push the shoulders back so that your back itself widens. A great way to do this is to lift your arms up. You'll probably feel that there's a gap between the floor and the shoulders. Keeping your arms up, press the shoulders back into the floor and then lower the arms.

You can place your hands on your abdomen and notice how your stomach rises and falls as you breathe in and out. Now think about your lower back. Think of yourself as a piece of wax, melting and spreading into the floor. Remember keep everything relaxed. Now, see if you can push your hips down towards your knees, whilst keeping the balls of your feet firmly fixed on the floor. You are aiming to lengthen and widen the whole of your back.

Move your focus onto the hands. Think about all the bones, release the tension in the wrists, and any tension in the fingers. Put your arms by your sides, being mindful of the shoulders. Think about your practice session, which areas have gone well. What do you need to focus on next?

It's also a great position to do some visualisation.
• Can you imagine yourself playing the notes that you've just practiced?
• Can you visualise the music in front of you?
• Can you imagine yourself holding your instrument? How does your posture look?
• Bring your arms into the playing position. How do your shoulders feel? Did they rise up as you adopted your playing position? If so, can you lower them again while in the playing position?

You want to stay in the semi-supine position for approximately 10 minutes. At first, this might seem like a lifetime. If necessary, start with 5 minutes and gradually increase the duration over a few weeks. You might feel sleepy at first which is normal. You may not be used to taking time out of your day to relax, but the more you do this, the more you'll feel energised when you get back up. When getting back up, do so slowly and carefully. Bring yourself gradually into an upright position, swivel your legs around and sit up on your knees. Lead with your head and then slowly, carefully re-align your spinal column until you are back in the standing position.

Lying in the semi-supine position is an excellent way to raise awareness of your body. The relaxed state that you experience on the floor is what you want to adopt when playing your instrument.

Your Feet

There are three balancing points in your feet, one on the heel, one on the ball of your big toe and the third on the ball of the little toe.

They form a triangle, and regardless of whether you sit or stand to play, these 3 points should be in contact with the floor.

People often place their weight unequally, so ask yourself do you naturally incline more to the right or the left? Do you lean more towards the heels or the balls of the feet? Do your feet roll inwards, or do they roll outwards? Very few people stand correctly with all three balancing points on the ground. The ground should feel like it's fully supporting you.

Balance

Our bodies are naturally balanced. To understand this, stand up and think about your feet, space your toes out. Think about the ball of your big toe and the ball of your little toe. Make sure you evenly distribute the weight between the two. Then think about your heels. Maybe you need to lean back a little bit more, make sure you're not arching your back. Keep the head forward and up, and then make sure you're not locking the knees. Relax the knees a little and sink the weight of your body into the floor. Your head should feel light and you shouldn't have any tension in the shoulders. If your shoulders are rounding forwards, think of pushing them backwards.

Now raise your arms midway, so they are level with your chest. If you're standing correctly, your body will go back slightly to keep you balanced when you raise your arms. Make sure you don't move from the hips or the pelvis. So *'no bottoms sticking out'* as my ballet teacher used to say.

As you lower your arms again, you'll notice your body moves slightly forward. If you play an instrument that you hold, the weight will affect your balance, and this needs consideration. You shouldn't compensate for this by lifting a shoulder, bending a knee or twisting the back.

Sitting to Play

If you sit to play be aware of your pelvis, make sure you sit equally on your *'sitting bones'*. Avoid pulling your weight forward, which often happens when playing the piano. Cellists, on the other hand, often lean too far backwards. If you rock from side to side, you should feel your 'sitting bones'. Slowly bring yourself back into the middle with equal weight on either side.

If there's one takeaway from this chapter, it's to enjoy the sense of movement in your body when you play. Don't try to play well, let your instrument become part of you. When we try too hard, it creates tension. Raise your awareness of what you are doing rather than the result that you're striving to achieve. And if you do that, you'll start to make progress more rapidly.

Chapter 8 - How The Brain Works

Understanding how the brain works will help you see why adopting good habits and practice methods matters. Most people know that repetition forms an essential part of practice, but they are often unaware why inaccuracies can be hard to eliminate. People often find that they can accomplish a section of music correctly in one session with practice, but when they try it again the next day, the errors reappear. It's all related to neural pathways and how your brain stores information. A lot of people do one of the following when they practice.

1. They start at the beginning and play until they get to their first major mistake. They fix the mistake and go over that part a few more times. Then, they carry on playing through the piece until they get to the next mistake, which they, once again, try to fix, and the whole process continues in this way. They use this method in every practice session.
2. They play from the beginning until they make a mistake. They fix the mistake. Then they start again from the beginning of the piece, play on through the mistake that they've corrected, and continue until they get to the next mistake. They will then go back to the beginning and repeat the whole process.
3. They take a small section and repeat it a certain number of times aiming to achieve as many accurate repetitions as possible, and then move on to another section.

All of the those methods are incorrect and, employing any one of them, might account for why your piece never reaches a high standard all the way through. So often, when I listen to people play they start well and then the accuracy goes downhill as the piece progresses. Many people end up in a situation where they can play the first page well, but the second page needs a lot more work. When you understand how the brain works, you'll realise why the methods outlined above give inconsistent results.

Before I continue, I want you to know that I'm not a neurologist, but I have studied plenty of research. If you want to go deeper and follow a more scientific approach, you'll find plenty of 'Ted Talks' on-line on the subject matter. However, for the purpose of this book, I've simplified things in the hope that it helps everyone gain a better understanding of how to practice effectively.

Inside the brain, we have information messengers, which are called neurons. Neurons transmit information to different parts of the brain and the rest of the nervous system. When we play a musical instrument, we use almost every part of the brain. There are few other activities which give the brain such a powerful workout. Science has shown that learning to play an instrument can even change the brains structure, keep it healthier and enable it to function better. It also improves your long term memory and many other skills. Hence, it's a really valuable and beneficial thing to do.

To play an instrument, we need many neurons to connect. It's a complex process which I won't go into. However, it's important to note that we have billions of neurons in the brain and throughout the body. The neurons send an electrical charge down a pathway, where specialised neurons called motor neurons, embedded in *muscle tissue, allow us to move and play the notes. This process* happens on every practice attempt, and our brain stores all of the information.

Transmitting the right information every time is important if you want to learn to play a piece that you can perform accurately on every occasion.

Imagine for a moment that you have two files in your brain, and there are different paths to each. In one corner is the file, let's call it the *Error* file where all your inaccurate attempts are stored. There are several pathways to get there because you've made various errors each time you practiced.

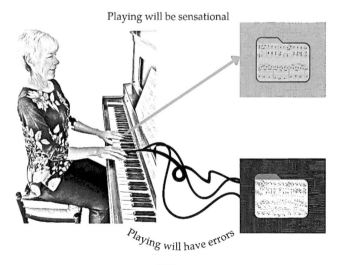

Playing will be sensational

Playing will have errors

In the other corner is your *Perfect* file, the file where you play amazingly; all your notes are accurate, the rhythm is precise, your tone is beautiful, and you shape the phrase with exquisite emotion. There is only one pathway to reach this point.

If I had to bet on which path you'd always choose to go down, it would be the green line to the *Perfect* file – right?

Now, let's look at what happens when you practise.

When you start at bar one and play to your first mistake, you create a path to your *Error* file. Even if you correct the mistake and carry on, you are still travelling along the path to that same file. You are strengthening that pathway by going further along it, or by repeating that same journey.

On your second attempt, you play with no errors and create a path – let's call it the *Green* pathway to the *Perfect* file. Fantastic, right? However, you now have two pathways, so on your third attempt there is a 50% chance that you'll take the path to your *Perfect* file, and a 50% chance you'll make errors. I think you'll agree 50/50 is not a great statistic to use in predicting which way things will go.

While the brain doesn't actually create files as such, it does create pathways and unfortunately, it stores every one of them. It can't delete them; they have to degrade, which takes a long time. Should you re-use a pathway, it's restored and considered necessary again, which is why, when repeating things with variable degrees of accuracy, you end up with unfavourable statistics. If you keep going back to the beginning of a piece, or phrase,in your practice sessions you will probably create more mistakes, and therefore add to your number of error pathways. Hence, the chances of you playing accurately weaken with each attempt. Let's say you've now had four attempts, three of which were incorrect, and one which was accurate. Based on this performance record, your chances of playing correctly on the fifth attempt are now just 25%.

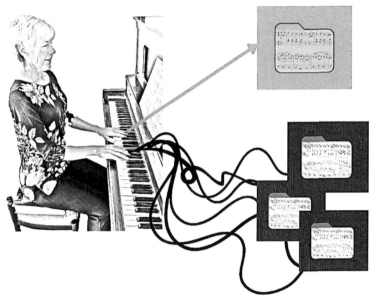

Hopefully, you can see that playing regularly, with repeated errors, is detrimental to your level of progress. So you are now probably thinking, how do I make sure that I always go down the *Green Pathway* to my *Perfect* file. Well, you have to strengthen the *Green Pathway*, and weaken the others. In future, once you've completed this book, I hope you'll know how to avoid creating any paths that lead to your *Error* file.

To strengthen a pathway, a process called myelination has to take place. Think of myelin as insulation that wraps around your neural pathways. It allows the information, in the form of electrical impulses, to supercharge its delivery speed. The more myelin you acquire, the more proficient you become at that action. We generate myelin through a process called myelination.

Myelination happens when you repeat something accurately, many times in a row. With each accurate repetition, the myelin thickens, and the information can travel faster. Your first accurate attempts require lots of concentration. Think of them like the old, slow dial-up way of connecting to the internet. Do you remember back in the late 1990s when you got a dialling tone and had to wait to connect to Internet Explorer? It was a slow and often frustrating process. With every accurate repeat you generate more myelin and the action becomes easier. When you have myelinated a pathway, it acts like fibre-optic broadband; Google opens immediately!

Myelinated pathways enable you to do actions without thinking about them. Walking is a great example. When you go for a stroll, you don't think about putting one leg in front of the other; the action happens automatically because those neural pathways have been myelinated.

We want to reach this stage with the piece that we're playing, so our fingers can do the actions with ease.

The most important thing is to STOP immediately when you make a mistake in your practice, and fix it. Don't be tempted to continue playing, even just a few notes. Once you've considered why the error occurred, start practising at the *exact point* where the mistake happened.

First, describe the error verbally to yourself, and then write it down in your practice diary. Remember that by writing it down, you are helping the brain to move that information into a more stable place. Describe what you need to do to correct the error. If it was a pitch error, ask yourself why that happened. Do you need to stretch your finger out further etc. I'll go into more detail on this in the Section entitled Perceive and Conquer.

The key takeaway from this chapter is to ask yourself - when you practice, are you strengthening (myelinating) the pathway to your Perfect file, or are you strengthening the pathway to your Errors file? If you've got an error in a piece which you just can't overcome, it's likely that you've myelinated that pathway. Unfortunately that error will be almost impossible to correct. The best option is to put the piece to one side for several months. Let the incorrect pathway degrade, and then practice in a more mindful and effective way next time around.

I'll talk more about how many times to repeat something in the chapter entitled Blocked Practice. Before I do though, let's look at what you should do at the start of each practice session to warm-up.

Chapter 9 - Warm-Up

If you were going to go for a run, you wouldn't hesitate to do some stretches beforehand. However, many people dive straight into the playing and consider scales and technical exercises to be enough preparation.

As I mentioned in the chapter on posture, you use lots of muscles to play your instrument, and it's essential to warm-up properly. It's also beneficial to quieten the mind before practising to ensure you are fully focused during your session. We all lead hectic lives and whether you think it or not, there are so many distractions in the modern world compared to ten years ago. Smartphones frequently ping with messages, then there are emails, social media etc. and we can't help but take a look, respond and reply *immediately*. Our minds are constantly in overdrive, and many of us are not even aware. We rarely take a few minutes to simply do nothing, to just relax and de-stress.

Often, we squeeze practice into our daily routine. Maybe you've been dashing around, just picked up the kids or gone grocery shopping. You get home with half an hour to spare before you need to start preparing dinner, so you squeeze in a bit of practice. The problem with this approach is your mind and body don't always focus on the task at hand. Perhaps you're thinking of what to cook or that item you forgot to buy while shopping, but at the same time, you are going through the motions of practice.

I'm sure you've had that experience before whereby you are carrying out an action, but your mind has been thinking about other things. Preparing the mind, before you begin your practice is *invaluable*. Take a few minutes to deep breathe, empty your head of thoughts and compose yourself, just as you would, for example, at the start of a yoga session.

Breathing exercises are a fantastic way to let go. Here's one that works wonderfully. You can also use this if you are getting frustrated during your practice or feel the need to refocus. Tension in our bodies often arises when we can't do something. When you find something a challenge, stop and take a few minutes to do this simple breathing exercise.

Exhale, through your mouth all the air in your lungs. Then breathe in through your nose over four counts, hold your breath for four counts and slowly exhale through your mouth for eight counts. You only need to do this a couple of times before you start to feel more relaxed. You'll find plenty more breathing exercises to use at the start of your practice by doing a quick google search. It's best not to begin practice until you feel calm, relaxed and focused.

Following on from the breathing exercises, take the time to do a quick body warm-up. Do a few shoulder rolls, followed by some circles with the neck. Get rid of the tension in the body. Stretch the arms and swing them around in a circle. A couple of minutes spent doing this will go a long way in helping your mind and body get in shape for your practice.

Injuries amongst musicians and athletes are not uncommon. Many stem from the lack of warm-up time and the amount of tension held in the body. It goes without saying that you want to avoid this at all costs. I suffered terribly from tendonitis whilst at music college and it's both debilitating and painful.

Warming up is something not to be skipped. It allows the mind and body to prepare so you can play at the highest level possible for your ability. In other words -

Warming up helps you reach your peak physical performance!

Warming up with the instrument.
It's not uncommon for learners to practise scales in their warm-up and/ or technical exercises. However, these are often done mindlessly and therefore serve little purpose. To be clear, I do believe that scales and technical exercises are of value, but only if your technique is good enough to be strengthened. When you understand why you are practising these scales and exercises, you know what to listen out for and how to make improvements, then they are very beneficial.

The simple exercise described below is one which I would encourage everyone to use at the start of their practice. If done with honest intentions, it will improve your playing and develop your technique with greater awareness and understanding.

Simple Exercise

The following **exercise is only beneficial if you really focus** on what happens in your body and pay attention to how your muscles feel.

Choose five consecutive notes on your instrument, and play them very slowly, going up and down. By not reading any music or worrying about the rhythm, you can focus solely on your muscle movements and how they impact the sound.

When you play these five notes, I want you to think about how high you're lifting your fingers away from the instrument and how the muscles feel in your hand?

- Can you feel any extra tension if you lift a finger higher, or does it feel better if you lower the finger more?
- Do you feel any pull or tension further up your arms?
- How do your shoulders react?
- Can you feel other muscles move in your body when you lift a finger?
- Is there more tension when the fingers are curved or flatter?

You are going to do this with each of your fingers. Think about curving them more or straightening them more. Ask yourself how the muscles feel and how does it affect the sound on your instrument. *Treat it like an experiment.*

Remember to move between the notes very slowly. I'm not asking you to do or change anything in your playing. I just want you to be thinking about how the tone sounds and how the muscles feel in your body. I do this exercise regularly, two or three times a day. At first, you may not notice anything. That's OK, after all it's not easy to purposely do less, or be really focused. If you *do this exercise daily, you will start to see a difference in your playing*. You'll become more aware of your body.

You are part of the instrument. It doesn't matter what instrument you play, guitar, saxophone, piano etc. Your body and instrument are one, and any tension, wherever it might be located, affects the sound that you make. So often, learners play in a tense way, especially when they're practising challenging music, or learning new patterns such as scales. Raising your awareness will help you improve. I hope you find the exercise as eye-opening as the participants did in the masterclass.

"The first time I practised the 5 notes, it was awful. No smoothness, notes wavering and generally poor. The second practice had great improvement; I was much more aware of my fingers on the keys." **Jonathan**

"I've been trying to get rid of a buzz when I play, and I discovered that if I release the tension, the buzz disappears. I've been trying for ages to get rid of it, and this exercise solved the problem. Thank you so much"- **Douglas**

So often, doing less helps us achieve so much more!

Following on from this simple exercise, I recommend doing two further warm-ups. One which focuses on scales, chords or arpeggios, but not in a traditional way, and the other that focuses on another aspect of your technique. I advise that you use material from the piece that you're learning instead of technical exercises and mindless scale practice.

Scale, Arpeggio or Broken Chord Warm-Up
You want to allocate 2 minutes to this part of your practice, and to help you stay focused I suggest setting a timer. We all focus more when we work against the clock.

Take one arpeggio or broken chord pattern from the piece that you are learning. If you are a beginner, you might not know what an arpeggio or chord is, but keep reading as I'll give you some ideas on this too. Sometimes arpeggios and chords are easy to spot in music, as they appear in the correct order. In the example below, you can see that the arpeggios follow the order 1, 3, 5 as you would expect to see them in a scale book. You are likely to find great examples of this in classical music, as composers such as Mozart often use scales and arpeggios in their compositions.

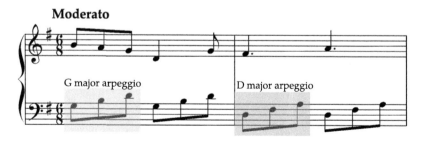

From J. S Fearis, Beautiful Isle of Somewhere, bars 5-6

You'll have to look more closely to spot such patterns in other pieces, as the notes may be mixed up. You can see in the example by Beethoven, below, that all the pitches of the G major, C major and A minor arpeggio are present but they do not appear in root position (the order 1, 3, 5).

From Beethoven, 6 Minuets woO 10 No 2 Minuet in G bars 13-16 of the trio

Beginners - Yo-Yo Exercise.

Put your metronome on 60 beats per minute and take the first two notes of your chosen arpeggio or chord. In the example below, I've used the C major arpeggio, so my first two notes are C and E. Playing one note per click, alternate between the notes C and E repetitively. See if you can keep the tone even, focus on the hand position and your posture on each attempt. After a few repeats, start to play the two notes in different octaves.

Remember to keep the tone even and the notes of equal volume. You can extend this exercise by playing the notes at different dynamic levels or varying articulation patterns.

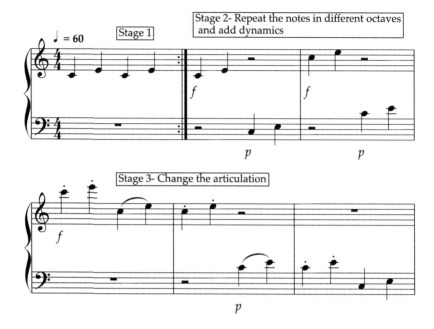

By moving around the instrument and incorporating alternative different dynamics and articulation patterns, you are familiarising yourself with the tonality of the notes and key while also incorporating other aspects of technique. You are also allowing yourself the space to focus on playing with a good tone. This is far more beneficial than just playing a C major arpeggio up and down with no real purpose. In your next practice session you can do the same thing but with the second and third notes of the arpeggio.

Next Step Up

Later in the week, practise a rhythm from your piece using the notes from your chosen arpeggio or chord. At this stage in your practice, you are not reading any music, so commit the rhythm and the notes of your arpeggio to memory. By not reading any music, you can focus more on listening to the sound you make, your posture and your hand position.

Tip!

If you struggle to remember the notes of a chord, write them down on a piece of paper and say them regularly throughout the day.

Intermediate Players

Creativity has an important place in music, so if you are an intermediate player you will want to use the notes of your chosen arpeggio or chord to improvise for a few bars. Explore the freedom of changing the order in which you play the notes and get creative with your rhythms. Initially, choose one rhythm and play it using the notes from your chord in any order or octave. Then gradually move away from that rhythm, maintaining the correct number of beats per bar and only using the notes of your chosen chord. Keep the metronome on to help you maintain a steady pulse. The more you explore the possibilities using only three notes in any octave, the more you'll familiarise yourself with the tonality. You'll gain a deeper level of focus and more awareness of the tone quality. You're also allowing yourself to be more creative musically.

134

Take the 3 arpeggio notes and improvise

Tip!

Keep the rhythms simple to begin with. For any music to sound 'good' it has to be rhythmic. People often think they can't improvise, but it's usually their lack of rhythmic precision which is the problem, not their ability to make up a melody. Less is always more when it comes to improvising.

Advanced Players.

Here are a few exercises to make the arpeggio patterns more challenging. You can do these at different dynamic levels and with varying patterns of articulation. Think about keeping your tone focused when you practice and ensure the finger coordination is neat.

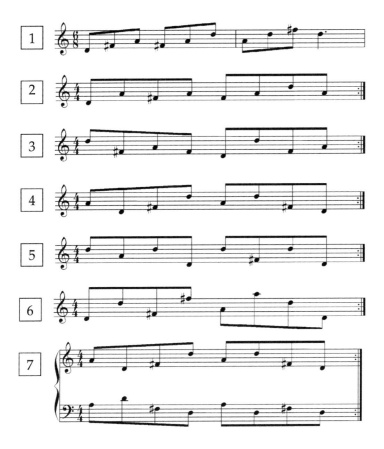

You can also use these exercises to develop your coordination on multi-lined instruments by playing in parallel or contrary motion, as shown in number 7.

As you continue through your practice session, you'll intersperse further scale practice, as changing tasks frequently heightens your focus. So let's take a look at the best ways to practise a scale.

Practising Scales

Again take a scale passage from the piece you are learning. Most pieces will include at least a small scale fragment, but if you are unsure, take the scale of the key that the piece is written in.

Memorising the notes of a scale.

Through my years of teaching, I know that people generally fall into one of two categories: those who can easily memorise scale patterns, and those who can't. For those who struggle to remember scales, I want to tell you that breaking down the patterns further and focusing on pieces in the same key does help. So let's say you are learning G major; make sure the pieces that you practice are also in the key of G until you fully grasp that pattern.

Start by writing the notes out in alphabet form on a piece of paper. All scale patterns follow the musical alphabet A B C D E F G. Of course, after the note G we return to A. So if a scale starts on D, the pattern will be D E F G A B C D. However, you need to remember which sharps or flats go alongside those letters. Writing a sentence such as *G major has an F sharp* in your practice diary is helpful. I am a firm believer that if you cannot say the notes in alphabet form, you do not honestly know the pattern. Remember, by writing things down, you are helping the brain store the information in a more stable place.

If you find scales challenging to remember, don't attempt to learn the whole scale at once. Begin with the first five notes, or even the first three notes if necessary. Practise saying the letter names regularly throughout your day and not just during your practice sessions.

Finger Patterns

Scales and finger patterns are closely related on string instruments and the piano. So it's worth writing out the finger pattern on a piece of paper and regularly saying the numbers alongside the letter names. For example: for G major on piano, practise saying,

1 on G, 2 on A, 3 on B, 1 on C and so on.

If you play a wind or brass instrument, include some kinaesthetic practice, where you mime the finger combinations. Once you can do this, see if you can imagine yourself playing those notes in your mind without going through the finger combinations with your hands.

Getting creative with your scales practice.

As I explained earlier, practising scale patterns up and down is OK, but it doesn't help you learn a piece. Rarely will you see a complete scale in your music. By being more creative with your scale practice, you'll familiarise yourself on a deeper level with the notes of that pattern. This leads to greater confidence in the execution. Here are a few more ideas to incorporate into your practice. If you don't play a single line instrument, try the following using each hand separately. Remember to only focus on one idea until you are proficient. Adults have a tendency to move on too soon. So, if you recognise this trait in yourself, be mindful of your actions, and resist the temptation to move on before you are ready.

Start the scale on different notes.

Within a piece of music, it's not uncommon to see a fragment of a scale that doesn't start on the tonic (first note). So often, learners don't connect the pattern and see only a set of ascending notes. If you practice your scale, starting on different notes, it will help you overcome this. You really don't need to practice all 8 notes so maybe, if you were practising G major, you could start on D and just play up to G.

Variations of Crabwise scales.

The following exercise is inspired by Crabwise scales, a pattern that more advanced musicians use to warm-up. Play the first five notes of the scale ascending, and then come down only four notes. Do this slowly and listen carefully to the tone, balance and intonation (if appropriate). You then go up five notes from the second note of the scale, and down four notes. Then go up five notes starting on the third note etc.

There are many variations you can use to make scale practice more fun and rewarding, whilst preserving the level of challenge. Moreover, by doing such methods, you'll understand that pattern at a much deeper level.

Practise a rhythm with the scale.

I mentioned this earlier in the chapter, but I want to reiterate it here, as it's a great way to combine two elements from your piece. Take a rhythm that you were learning yesterday and use it to practise your scale.

Practise with a scale backing track.

One of my recommendations for developing your musical foundations is to practise your scale with a backing track. Playing along with an accompaniment develops your rhythmic skills, inner ear, listening skills, aural skills, and musicality, to name but a few of the benefits. However, for most people, it means they have to step outside their comfort zone.

To begin with, you can keep things simple. Take three notes from your scale and just play them as semibreves (whole notes) consecutively up and down. Then change the order of these notes as you begin to gain confidence. You can add further notes and use more interesting rhythms as you progress.

There are lots of scale backing tracks on YouTube. Most are aimed at guitarists, but it doesn't matter, you can use them whatever instrument you play. The only thing to bear in mind if you play a transposing instrument such as clarinet, trumpet or saxophone, is the interval of transposition. See the table on the next page for the first few keys to get you started.

	Key of backing track to play along to for transposing instruments.			
Scale you are practising on your instrument	In the key of C piano, harp, flute oboe, trombone, cello, violin, guitar	In the key of Bb Trumpet, clarinet, tenor saxophone	In the key of Eb Alto saxophone, tenor horn, alto clarinet	In the key of F French horn, English horn
C Major	C Major	Bb Major	Eb Major	F Major
F Major	F Major	Eb Major	Ab Major	Bb Major
G Major	G Major	F Major	Bb Major	C Major
Bb Major	Bb Major	Ab Major	Db Major	Eb Major
D Major	D Major	C Major	F Major	G Major
A Minor	A Minor	G Minor	C Minor	D Minor
D Minor	D Minor	C Minor	F Minor	G Minor
E Minor	E Minor	D Minor	G Minor	A Minor
G Minor	G Minor	F Minor	Bb Minor	C Minor
B Minor	B Minor	A Minor	D Minor	E Minor

Note: Minor backing tracks are usually for the natural version of the scale. If you want to practice the harmonic version, be sure to add that when you search for example, backing track for D harmonic minor.

To find a backing track, type into YouTube the name of the scale followed by the words *backing track*. You're likely to get lots of results in different styles, so you can practice along to different ones each day.

For many, the prospect of improvising along to a backing track is daunting, and it's easy to say *that's not for me.* Remember those adult fears? One of the first things my nephew does when he visits is ask if he can *play on the piano.* He's seven years old and doesn't take piano lessons, but he is intrigued by the sounds that he can create. It's interesting to watch him explore the different timbres and to see how he improvises his little melodies. Unlike an adult, he isn't judging himself by the result; he's just enjoying his own music. If you can find that inner child within you, the sky's your limit. Start simply by playing long notes going up and down the scale. It may take months before you have the confidence to start improvising your own melodies; that's ok and completely normal. The more you can explore being free with your music, the more significant the impact will be on your musicality.

Second Warm-Up Exercise
There are so many things that you can do for your second warm-up exercise. It really depends on what piece you are learning and what level of ability you have. The idea here is to focus on another aspect of technique that you'll need to play the piece you are learning. You might create exercises to practice intonation, ornamentation, double stops, pedalling, spacial awareness across large leaps, tonguing etc.

The following examples will not apply to all instruments, but the aim is to give you some inspiration and ideas. You can access a video in which I personally demonstrate some of these techniques in the extra resources for this book which are available at playmusicbetterbook.com/resources.

Large Leaps or Shifts in Position

Take two notes or chords and practise them individually, make sure the tonal focus is in the centre and the intonation is reliable. Now mime the change in position. As you do this, think about which muscles need to move, and then be aware of that muscle movement in advance. So, as you play the first note, imagine your hand moving to the position of the second note. Then try and play the shift slowly. Ask yourself *if any finger is moving slower than the others, is the rotation of the hand position correct, are you holding any tension as you change position?* Repeat the exercise until you can shift or move between the two notes fluently and with ease.

A Sequential Passage

A sequence is a pattern of notes which repeats higher or lower. Below you can see that the intervals repeat going through the octaves.

You could create a warm-up exercise whereby:

Firstly, you play the notes F and C across the whole range of the instrument. As you're doing this, make sure you are aware of how your arms cross and listen to the tone to ensure it remains even. Take care not to place too much weight on the first note as you cross your hands. Start slowly and use a metronome to avoid any gaps or hesitations, especially when you cross the hands. On day two, you could do the same thing, but with the intervals of a fourth. Then later in the week, you could alternate them as in the original bar. You could also repeat the intervals using different rhythms or focus on repeating the two notes of the interval to improve the intonation.

Chord Progressions for Beginners

Coordination is one of the challenges when playing chords. Creating a warm-up exercise whereby you play the notes individually, then add a rest before playing the chord together helps. The rest is important as it gives you the space and time to coordinate the fingers and play the notes together, simultaneously. You might start with a long rest, and throughout your practice, make the rest shorter and shorter until you can play the chord with ease. You should aim to improve something every time you repeat it. At first that might mean focusing on a particular finger, then moving on to focus on the balance of the chord, making sure the tone production of the notes is even. Listen carefully to the intonation and make sure that there is no tonal blemish that you need to address. If your piece has a melody which is supported by chords, it makes sense that you should be able to play the chord progression fluently before complicating it with a melody.

You can see in the example below that the left hand has intervals of a 5th throughout. Whilst the intervals are mixed up in the piece itself, you could create an exercise by writing them out in ascending order. You might need to focus on the hand position, shifts or the coordination. Perhaps you practise just the first two open fifths on day one, and as the week progresses, you add more of the chords.

From Ravenscroft's Deuterumedia, Anon, Loath to Depart bars 4-6

Left hand intervals written in descending order

Exercise to practice the left hand

Here's another example with different chords. Again take out the chords and write the progression out as long notes. Notice the spatial awareness needed in the hands for each chord. Familiarise yourself with the fingering by repeating each chord change until you can do it with ease. Try and memorise the passage. Perhaps verbalise the chord pattern so you recap it several times, vocally, throughout the day.

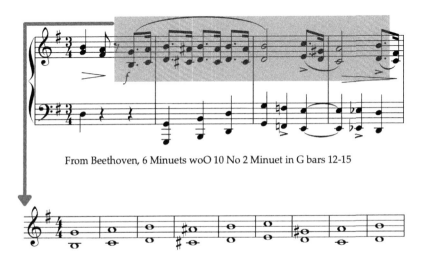

From Beethoven, 6 Minuets woO 10 No 2 Minuet in G bars 12-15

Ornaments

Musical ornaments rarely get the practice they deserve. Their purpose is to decorate a melody, yet they frequently do anything *but*. It's often worth writing ornaments such as trills or turns, in full on manuscript paper. So often, people play trills without thinking about how many repetitions they'll make between the two notes. I always like to remind my students that ornaments should *decorate*, not *dominate*. You can apply this motto to other decorative elements too, such as pitch bends. Remember, the melody is always the most important part. Everything else comes second because, without a melody, a piece of music loses its *sense* of character.

From Mozart Clarinet Quintet K.V. 581, first movement, bars 182-184

Taking ornaments to one side and practising them, will help you gain control and precision. It's always wise to slow the ornament down and practise with a metronome. Decide how the left hand (if appropriate) will coordinate with a trill, for example, and gradually build up the repetitions, ensuring that the tonal control and finger coordination remain even. You can gradually increase the speed and measure your progress over the current and subsequent, practice sessions.

On the next page you'll see some examples of how I would encourage you to practice ornamental passages such as the example above by Mozart.

Step 1- Practice the bars without the trills

Step 2- Add the trill to beats 1 and 3

Step 3- Add the trill to beats 2 and 4

Step 4- Practice the bars slowly in full

148

Yo-Yo Between Two Notes

If you've got any awkward finger patterns to coordinate or you want to improve the intonation between two notes, this exercise works well. Play the two notes slowly, using a tuning machine if necessary. Think about your posture, breath support, bow hold, or whatever it might be and aim to improve the quality of the notes with each repetition. As you gain more confidence, start to gradually increase the speed, always ensuring your tonal control remains excellent.

Yo Yo exercise

etc

Pedalling

Overuse of the pedal is common amongst learners, and few understand its real purpose. The main purpose of the damper pedal on a piano (the right pedal) is to manipulate the tone. It is not to play legato, except when it is not possible to connect the notes using a legato touch. Legato phrasing should be done with your fingers and not with the pedal. The damper pedal gives the piano's tone more resonance and depth. If you have pedal marks in the piece you are learning, think carefully about where you will put the pedal down and where you'll lift it up. Vocalise the pedal movement with the notes.

From Schubert, Impromptu in Ab, D.935 (Op.142) No.2 bars 1-3

Pedal down play the Eb
pedal up change the chord

Note: you still hold the Ab when using the pedal

Start by playing the right hand with the pedal, then try the left hand by itself with the pedal. When you can coordinate the pedal with each hand separately, slowly try both hands together. Listen carefully and make sure there is no blemish in the tone as a result of inaccurate pedal movements.

Chapter 10 - Rhythm

"There is music wherever there is rhythm, as there is life wherever there beats a pulse." **Stravinsky**

Music is nothing without rhythm. It's the driving force behind any piece or song, in a similar way that an engine is to a car. Yet, it's something that most learners don't fully understand. Sure, they know that a crotchet (quarter note) is worth one, but what that *relates to* is the part that's often not fully grasped. When you genuinely understand rhythm, and you can align it with the beat, a magical transformation happens in the music.

When Rolf joined my 'Learn Music Together' Academy, he was a reasonably able player. He was a church organist who had played in a brass band throughout his life and regularly sang in a choir. Hence he was no stranger to giving a concert. However, he was struggling to take his playing to the next level. It became apparent through our conversations that he had never really practised with a metronome. He had taken lessons throughout his life and thought that his sense of rhythm was not too bad. No one had told him any differently, and he had never considered the difference that complete rhythmic precision would make. He started implementing my methods and began to understand the importance of rhythm. This is what he had to say:

"I was at two concerts and it occurred to me that both professional organists had a lack of rhythm in their overall performance. For

instance, I compared a Bach Triosonate to a piece on YouTube, and I got it! With much better rhythm, the music suddenly dances and gets much more interesting to listen to. That's certainly something I have to focus on myself." **Rolf**

I remember that, as a child, most of my music teachers told me to practice with a metronome, but no one ever taught me how to do that. Nor did they explain what rhythm and beat actually mean. That was until I went to college and studied with Richard Ingham. I was learning *Brazileira*, the third movement of *Scaramouche by Milhaud*. I can remember Richard explaining how the saxophone part had to align perfectly with the semiquavers (sixteenth notes) in the accompaniment, but I couldn't get it right. At some point in the lesson, it became apparent that I didn't fully grasp the concept of rhythm and beat. The rest of the session was spent setting up the groove and learning how to use the metronome in various ways to achieve precision. Once I gained that clarity, I, like Rolf, realised that rhythm is what makes music. You can get away with playing the occasional wrong note if the rhythm is accurate, but it doesn't work the other way round. If you play all the right notes, but they aren't all in the right place, the music never truly dances.

So many adult learners run into difficulty with rhythm because of one big mistake.

Are you ready?

When people are practising, they try and do all things at once. What I mean by that is, they dive straight in and attempt to play the music with:

• The right notes
• Correct rhythm
• Coordination of both hands
• Fantastic tone and correct articulation.

Attempting everything at once is a recipe for disaster, and the level of accuracy is more often than not compromised. The one thing that every piece of music relies upon is a strong sense of rhythm. Rhythm isn't approximate: it is mathematical. The beat in music is an essential ingredient that has to be carefully measured. Now we all know that the metronome is the tool to ensure our music beats stay in time. But that adds another layer of complexity when we practice. The continuous ticking can be annoying, but most of all, the reality that we are not playing in time is what frustrates many even if they are yet to admit it.

This is when they commit the **BIG mistake** which you have to avoid at all cost: **They turn the metronome off!** You wouldn't be the first person to tell me that you play better without the metronome, because the ticking puts you off. However, the only person you are cheating is yourself. Those metronome clicks are putting you off because they are telling you that your timing is out. That's hard to accept, but it is the truth.

Trust me, avoid the temptation to practise without a metronome because:

1. When you learn rhythms incorrectly, it's so much harder to correct them.
2. Your music will slow down at the difficult points, or even worse, it will lack fluency.
3. You'll find it challenging to gain the confidence to play the piece all the way through.
4. Turning the metronome off DOES NOT solve your problems with rhythm.

But most of all, it will take you much longer to gain proficiency and fluency in your music-making, which, in turn, may lead to a lack of motivation and slower progress for you, on your musical journey. The sooner you see the benefits of the metronome, the sooner you'll start to make better progress. Prevention is always better than cure, so let's look at how you can make the metronome your best friend, rather than your enemy. This is totally possible, when you know how.

What is a beat in music?

When I ask this question, people often reply with 'a crotchet' or 'it's one count,' both of which are not entirely true. A beat is a unit in time. Think of a clock for a moment. One second is a beat; one minute is a beat; one hour is a beat. For those beats to become meaningful, you need to know *what they are in relation to*. The big hand on a clock beats 60 times every hour. The second-hand beats 60 times every minute. The number on a metronome relates to the number of ticks you will hear per minute. For example, if you put your metronome on 60, it will click 60 times in one minute. That's one click per second. If the metronome is clicking at 120 beats per minute, that's two clicks per second. The value of a beat in music is defined by the time signature, which I'll come to shortly.

What is the pulse in music?
The pulse is the frequency of the beats. Like your heartbeat, the beats in music need to be equal and consistent. If your heart starts to beat with an irregular pulse, the likelihood is you'll need hospital treatment. For many, the solution is to have a pacemaker fitted. Think of a metronome as your pacemaker when practising. Without it, your music will not be fully 'fit.'

> **Note:** Tapping your foot is not a replacement for a metronome. You will conveniently, and without realising it, slow down or speed up, depending on how easy or challenging you find the passage.

Exercise: How the pulse varies so easily
To see how consistent your internal sense of pulse is, try this exercise. You'll need a device, such as a phone, or a tablet, to record yourself on. You are going to record yourself counting to 10 at a speed of 1 per second. Say the first two counts out loud, and then silently count from 3 to 10 in your head. On the 11th second, clap your hands.

Now, play back the recording and repeat the exercise. If you keep the pulse exactly the same, you should clap your hands precisely at the same time. If you repeat the exercise several times, the likelihood of you clapping simultaneously on every attempt is slim.

To develop your sense of pulse, try this next exercise. You'll need a friend to help, or you can get access to some exercises in the extra resources for this book.

I call this exercise 'Feel the Beat' and it is great fun to do with all the family. Clap the beat along to some music on the radio. Ideally, you want to do this to a song that has a strong pulse: something like, *'We will Rock You'* by Queen or a classical march, for example. When you're comfortable clapping along, get a friend to turn the volume off for a few bars while you keep clapping the beat. When your friend turns the volume back on, ask yourself if you've sped up or slowed down.

What is tempo in music?

The tempo of a piece indicates how fast or slow the music beats need to go. Remember, they still need to beat consistently and equally. Again it's like your heartbeat; if you go for a run, your heart rate will increase, but those beats will still be equally distanced. The tempo is either given by a metronome mark in which case you already have the number of beats per minute, or it's given by a word. Common musical terms that indicate the tempo include Lento, Andante, Moderato, Allegro and Presto. There are, however, many more. Metronomes will sometimes give an indication of what speed to use for the Italian terms. I've included an example of such, below, for your reference.

Suggested metronome speeds for Italian tempo markings	
Italian term	**Metronome Mark**
Largo	40-60
Larghetto	60-66
Adagio	66-76
Andante	76-108
Moderato	108-120
Allegro	120-168
Presto	168-208

What is rhythm in music?

Rhythm is a pattern of long and short sounds. The value of these sounds is defined by the value of the beat. For most learners, this is where the confusion begins. Most music tutor books begin by telling you that a crotchet has the value of one beat, which is true if the time signature is 2/4, 3/4 or 4/4. However, if the time signature is 2/2, then the value of a crotchet (quarter note) is a half, not one. I'm going to pause this conversation here and return to it once I've explained my method of attaining rhythmical precision when you practise.

How to practise the rhythm of your piece.

Unless you are confident with using a metronome, you should avoid subdivision when learning a piece. Instead, take the shortest note value in the music and use that as your beat. In the music below, the shortest note value is a quaver (eighth note) so you would count in quavers when you practise.

Count in the shortest notes value

From Bartók, For Children, No. 20 Stay Home, Hanulienka, bars 1-4

To help you achieve rhythmical accuracy, I have a four-step process to follow:

1. First, say the counts to a metronome. If need be, write the counts on the music. The more you do this, the quicker you will gain precision. Remember, we process things better when we write them down and vocalise them.

2. Keep things simple to begin with. Forget about adding up the beats in the bar to the time signature. Count everything individually. If the shortest note value in your piece is a quaver (eighth note), you will need to hold a crotchet (quarter note) for 2 counts because there are 2 quavers in a crotchet. I would encourage you to say '1 hold," rather than

158

'1, 2.' By saying '1 hold,' you are reaffirming to yourself what you will do when you play. If you say '1, 2,' you are likely to play on 2, when you should be holding. Start by putting your metronome on 60. The click will represent the shortest note value in your piece. In the previous example, this will mean the click represents a quaver (eighth note). So my metronome is clicking at a speed of 60 quaver beats per minute.

If you need a helping hand with rhythmic units, let me introduce you to a note pyramid. These are a fantastic way of understanding rhythmic subdivisions.

Note Pyramid

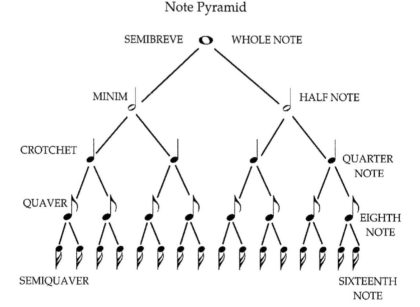

3. When you can say the rhythm to a metronome, the next step is to clap the rhythm. When you are clapping, continue to say the counts out loud. For a crotchet (quarter note), hold your hands together for the second click. Practise clapping the rhythm, until you can do it accurately several times in a row. Clap through it more times than you think is necessary.

4. Now choose a note on your instrument, and play the rhythm on that one note. If your instrument allows, say the counts out loud. If that's not possible, say the counts in your head. This is an important step. It's like a *'halfway house,'* as you're asking your brain to play your instrument, but you are not asking it to coordinate the fingers and read the music. Hence it gives you more *head-space* to focus on the rhythm. You'll then use one of the methods in chapter 12 to put the right notes to the rhythm.

Keep counting in the shortest note values when you learn new pieces until you can complete the process easily. This will be when you can say the rhythm, clap the rhythm and play the rhythm on one note accurately on your first attempt.

It may take you many months to get to this stage; just know that this is OK. If you put the hard work in now, you'll go a lot further in the long run. You can play a lot of music at a reasonably fast tempo without worrying about any subdivision. Although at this stage, I would avoid music with note values shorter than a quaver (eighth note).

Rests in Music

While quotes, such as that below, (which is often attributed to Mozart and similar variants to composers such as Debussy),

"The music is not in the notes, but in the silence in between"

are easy to find on the internet, they are unlikely to have been written by such greats, as there is no source evidence. However, there is some truth in the words.

Silence has great power in music; it creates tension, suspense and provides a contrast to the sound of the notes. It can be subtle, have complex qualities, or be dramatic and bold. Silence in the middle of a piece can pique your audience's curiosity, while the silence at the end leaves them wanting more.

Whether Mozart is the author of the above quote or not, silence allows the music to breathe. In many ways, the music takes place not on the beats but rather in the time between the beats. Learners are often intimidated by silence, and it's not uncommon for rests to be rushed and the following beat to be anticipated. Rests, just like notes, need practice, and you should treat them in the same way. I like to encourage learners to say the word rest when they vocalise the counts. If it's a two-beat rest, say rest rest, making sure you pronounce the letter R with each click of the metronome. When clapping, do an action with your hands, such as opening them apart to help you be more physically aware of the silence.

Silence has been an important structural element of numerous works, none more famous than John Cage's 4'33". That piece causes as much controversy today as it did when it premiered in 1952. In case you haven't come across the work, the performer walks on stage, sits at the piano and does various things like open a book, or adjust the stool. The whole event is timed for precisely four minutes and thirty-three seconds, and not a note of music is played. Cage was making the point that there is no such thing as silence. There are always sounds within a space - but only those who genuinely listen can hear them. Whatever you think of music that pushes the boundaries in such ways, there is an incredible amount of tension created in a room when you sit in silence for even a short amount of time, and tension always builds emotion. Music is, for many people, a way of expressing emotion, wouldn't you agree?

Developing an internal sense of pulse.
It feels amazing when you can keep time with a metronome, and your playing will already sound more musical. However, you now have to develop the skill of maintaining time *without* a metronome. Please note you should only attempt this next step when you can play your piece in time using a metronome.

The brain acts differently when you turn the metronome off, which is why some people can keep time with an external device but not without. So assuming you can stay in time with a metronome, the following exercise is an excellent way to develop your internal sense of pulse.

Set the metronome to click on every other beat. To do this, you will need to halve the metronome mark. For most people, this change is too dramatic to get good results as it requires you to then subdivide. A more effective way is to use an app such as *Time Guru Metronome*. There is a small fee for the app, but it's not much and certainly worth the investment.

When you open the app, don't bother with setting the number of beats per bar etc. Simply put in the metronome mark that you require, and then you will use the *random mute* feature to silence some of the beats. Slide the bar that says random mute to 10% and toggle on the gradual mute.

Time Guru Metronome

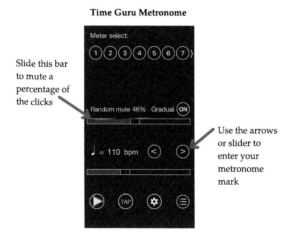

Slide this bar to mute a percentage of the clicks

Use the arrows or slider to enter your metronome mark

When you turn on the metronome, it will start by clicking every beat and gradually silence 10% of the beats. You'll know when you are maintaining time if your beats align with the metronome clicks that *do* sound. Once you have achieved this with 10% of the beats silenced, you can gradually increase the random mute all the way to 90%.

Chapter 11 - Developing Rhythm

Adults love to rush ahead, and it's not many authors that would tell you to skip a chapter. However, if you still can't play one note per click with a metronome, I'd love you to go straight to chapter 12. You can come back to this chapter at a later date. It'll still be here, and you'll be ready to take action.

Subdivsion

Only when you are confident that you can play one note per click accurately should you start to consider subdivision. Even then, I would start with only subdividing beats by two. There are several ways that you can count subdivisions; personally, I like to use words. At this stage, I think it's still essential to count in individual units. In other words, don't worry about the time signature, and which beats are strong or weak. I have my reasons for this, and it's probably the most controversial aspect of this book. However, few learners consider weak and strong beats when they play, nor can they play in time with a metronome. For those things to happen, you have to understand how the rhythms in music relate to each other *mathematically*. You can count a crotchet as 1, 2 or 4, if you count your other note values accordingly. Hence if you determine the value of a crotchet (quarter note) to be 2, then the value of a quaver (eighth note) is 1. Similarly, if a minim (half note) has the value of 1, a crotchet has the value of a half.

Back to subdivision. I like to use the word *coffee,* whenever I'm teaching how to divide a beat by 2 to a metronome. The first syllable, *Cof,* comes with the click, and the second syllable, *fee* comes halfway between the first and second click. It's a good idea to record yourself at this stage, to check your accuracy. See if you can record yourself vocalising the counts to the phrase below. Set a crotchet (quarter note), equalling 60, on a metronome. Give yourself a four count lead in, so that you can align your recording with the metronome in part two of this exercise.

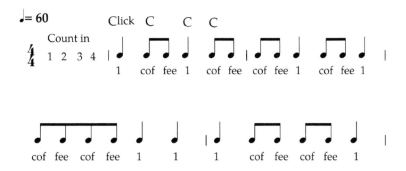

Now when you listen back to your recording, put your metronome on 120. This will give you the quaver (eighth note) speed, and see if you say the syllables *cof* and *fee* on the recording, with the metronome clicks at 120.

Continue to use the same process that I outlined in chapter 10 - say the rhythm, clap the rhythm, and play the rhythm on one note. If you struggle to subdivide the beats evenly, go back to *'counting in'* the shortest note values.

When you can confidently subdivide two beats to a metronome click, you can start to consider the time signature. At this stage, you should still be focusing on music which doesn't use note values shorter than a quaver (eighth note).

Dotted Crotchet (Dotted Quarter Note) Rhythm

If there is one rhythm that learners find challenging, when they progress to counting only the main beats of the bar, it's the dotted crotchet (dotted quarter note). In **2/4, 3/4** and **4/4**, a dotted crotchet is worth one and half beats mathematically. The challenging part to understand is that the half beat is the first part of beat number 2.

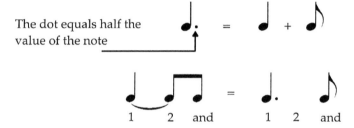

The dot equals half the value of the note

To help you gain accuracy, start by saying 'one click and one.' You'll say the word 'click' with the metronome click on the second beat; then you have to fit the word 'and' in between the second and third clicks so that you say 'one' with the third click.

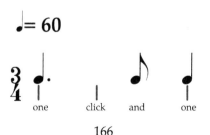

166

Tip!

If you find that you want to play as you say the word 'click,' replace it with the word hold, so, 'one hold and one.'

Tied Notes

Often, learners anticipate the following beat *after* a tied note, just like they do with rests. When you're counting in the smallest note values, this is usually less of a problem, but when you progress to subdivision, it's something to be aware of. In the following example, the second quaver is tied over to the following beat; the tie itself poses no problem, but often learners will play the next beat early.

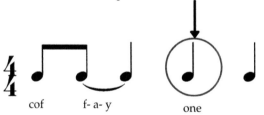

Take care not to anticipate the beat after a tied note.

cof   f- a- y   one

I recommend extending the word, *coffee*, when vocalising the counts to *'coffaay'* to remind yourself to hold the second quaver. Then, focus on ensuring you say the *word, one,* with the next metronome click.

Time Signatures

The time signature has an important role in transforming the rhythm in music. The two numbers at the start of the piece tell you which beats in the bar should be strong and which should be weak.

Time signatures fall into three categories.

- **Simple**
- **Compound**
- **Irregular**

Within the first two categories, you have further subsections which define the number of beats.

- **Duple- meaning there are two beats in a bar**
- **Triple- meaning there are three beats in a bar**
- **Quadruple- meaning there are four beats in a bar**

You can also have quintuple, septuple, and in contemporary music, many more time signatures. However, I'll stick to the most common ones for the purposes of this book.

The subsections are often omitted when time signatures are first described in a tutor book, and again, it's something that I think causes confusion later. Most people are taught that the top number of a time signature tells you how many beats there are in a bar. The bottom number tells you what type of beats they are. This information is correct, but when taught in this way, it doesn't inform a student where the strong and weak beats are.

Duple Time

2/4 2/2, 6/8 are all duple time signatures. They all have two beats in a bar. The first beat is strong and the second beat is weak. When you play a piece in these time signatures, you should give an accent to the first beat of each bar. We call this first beat the downbeat.

Triple Time

3/8, 3/4, 3/2, 9/8 are all examples of triple time signatures. They all have three beats in a bar. The first beat is strong while the second and third are weak beats. You should accent the downbeat (the first beat) and not beats two and three in each bar.

Quadruple Time

4/4, 4/2, 12/8 are all quadruple time signatures. The accents in these time signatures *go* strong, weak, medium, weak. When you don't lean on the downbeats, the rhythmical energy of a piece is suppressed. Think back to Rolf's earlier words, *the rhythm dances.*

Let's look at a piece in **2/2** for a moment. The time signature **2/2** has two minim beats per bar. *The value of minim should be one beat, and the beats should go **strong, then weak.*** When you first practice the piece, you would probably count in crotchets (quarter notes) which is fine initially, but it won't give the music the correct feel. Why? Because the accents (strong and weak beats) will be misplaced or not considered. Once you can play the piece at a reasonable speed, you need to change the way you count so that you can focus on accenting the downbeat.

From Beethoven, 5 Military Marches, No2 WoO 19, bars 1-4

Another time signature that is often not fully grasped is **6/8.** The definition of **6/8** is two dotted crotchets (dotted quarter notes) per bar. It's a compound duple time signature, meaning that there is one strong beat in the bar and one weak beat.

Without that information, a learner thinks that **6/8** is 6 quavers in a bar. There are indeed 6 quavers in a bar, but the main beats are dotted crotchets (dotted quarter notes). If you clap the beat to a piece of music in **6/8** you should clap twice per bar, not six times. Unlike **3/4** which also has 6 quavers in a bar, but in this time signature there are 3 beats in a bar. Music written in **6/8** has a completely different feel to music in **3/4.** Why? Because of the strong and weak beats.

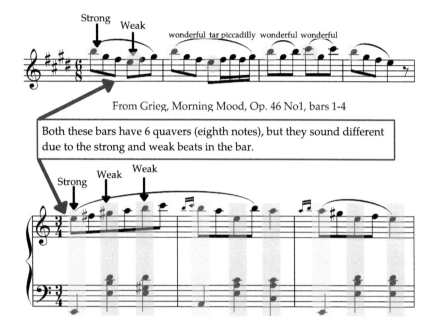

From Grieg, Morning Mood, Op. 46 No1, bars 1-4

Both these bars have 6 quavers (eighth notes), but they sound different due to the strong and weak beats in the bar.

From Chopin, Waltz No 19 in A Minor, B 150 bars 17-19

Getting the correct rhythmic feel in your playing is challenging. It's at this stage that learners often lose rhythmic precision. You have to, firstly, be able to play one note per click on a metronome before you can attempt subdivision. When subdividing, you need to focus on making sure the right notes align with the metronome clicks. Again vocalising the counts, then clapping the rhythm, then playing the rhythm on one note will really help. Build the phrase up very slowly when you add in the correct notes. Start by playing the first beat in full and stop on the first note of the second beat so you can hear whether you land with a click on the metronome. Record yourself so that you can listen back.

How do you practice leaning on the downbeat?

Once you can play your piece, and keep time with a metronome, you can use an app such as Tempo Metronome to silence the weak beats in a bar. You can, then, practice emphasising beat 1 with the metronome click.

J.S. Bach, Notebook for Anna Magdalena, BWV Anh 132, Menuet in D Minor bars 1-4

Tricky Rhythms and Syncopation

The easiest way to ensure that you play complex rhythms accurately is to write the bar out with double the note values. Practise counting in the smallest note values and then gradually increase the metronome speed in increments of 4 or 5.

From Debussy, Children's Corner, VI Golliwogg's Cakewalk, bars 10-11

Tip- Double the note values for slow accurate practice

When you can play the passage proficiently, and can't go any quicker on the metronome, half the metronome mark and start the process again, this time counting in the correct beat for the time signature.

Syncopated rhythms are challenging as they require you to play off the beat. Here's a simple syncopated exercise to practice: you could do this in your warm-up. If you play in a band, you may have come across a few bars that look like this. I like to use the words *Oom Pah*, to help gain rhythmic precision. Start with the metronome on 60 for a crotchet beat. Say the word *Oom* with the click, and *pah* inbetween the clicks.

173

Chapter 12 - Slow Practice

'Just listen, please don't play.'
'Stop at exactly the point I told you to, don't go on.'
'Think in between your practice attempts.'

I say these sentences frequently when I'm teaching adults.
They are so eager to learn and try, yet they fail to understand
that by not listening and engaging fully in what they are
playing, they are making things way harder for themselves.

Slow practice is much more than just practising your pieces at
a slow tempo. It's about fully immersing yourself within every
session. Just like slow travel emphasises the connection
between local people, culture, food and traditions, so slow
practice emphasises the connection between all musical
elements. It relies on the idea that effective practice is meant to
educate and have emotional impact, not just in the present
moment, but in a form which you may carry into the future.
One of the most challenging concepts for adult learners to take
on board is that slow practice involves *thinking more* and
playing less.

Have you ever experienced starting your piece, for example,
on the wrong note? You're not alone if you have. It's an error
that happens to many learners. They brush it off, as if it didn't
happen, and immediately start again. However, it should
never happen in the first place if you take your time and think
before you play.

Practising at a slower pace has many benefits. It eliminates errors, confusion, silly mistakes, and it develops greater control. When you slow down, you have time to fine-tune the execution, identify errors and find creative solutions. Your mind should experience a physical workout, and when you fully engage in the process, it helps the brain store the information in the long term memory.

With every note you play, you should strive for accuracy. As you repeat the phrase or the bar, you should seek to improve the outcome. Here are a few ideas to think about.

1. **Rhythm**. Are you aligning the notes with the metronome?
2. **Tone**. Is the tone warm, even and focused?
3. **Intonation**. Are all the intervals beautifully placed?
4. **Balance.** Is the melody projected or suitably supported?
5. **Posture.** Are you sitting or standing correctly. Is your breath flowing with ease? How relaxed are your shoulders?
6. **Phrasing**. Are you shaping the phrase, and keeping the phrase contours refined?
7. **Articulation.** Is the staccato crisp, or the legato smooth? Is your articulation in keeping with the style? Is the tone remaining focused when you articulate the notes?
8. **Dynamics.** Do the notes sound at the right dynamic level? Have you got the tonal colours right?
9. **Tension.** Are you playing in a relaxed way, or are you tensing any part of your body?

In between your physical practice, you should take the time to practice the notes in your mind. Imagine how it feels to play the notes. What fingers are you using to play the notes, can you recall what the pitches are, what the rhythm is, and, ultimately, can you hear how you want a phrase to sound?

At first, you may think that you are achieving very little. Maybe you think it's dull, or you find it frustrating. It's normal to feel this way, but that doesn't mean you should stop and revert to your old methods. *Slow* practice is the way to *faster* progress.

If you are getting frustrated, take a break, and remember to keep practice sessions short. Always plan your sessions ahead of time, and write down what you've achieved. Stop focusing on the end result. Practice is not about reaching perfection; it's about the improvements you are making. If you keep this at the forefront of your mind, you will find that practicing is rewarding, uplifting and highly motivating.

Kinaesthetic Practice

Kinaesthetic learning combines your visual and/or auditory senses. It's a great way to achieve a higher level of accuracy when you practise. There are many things that you could do to help you consolidate the music in your brain. We've already discussed clapping through the rhythms, but here are a few other suggestions to consider before you physically practice the phrase you are learning.

1. Read through the letter names until you can say them fluently.

2. Read through, or mime the finger co-ordinations necessary to play the notes.
3. Vocalise the rhythm and mime the finger combinations.
4. Sing the melody while clapping the rhythm.
5. Sing the melody while miming the finger combinations.
6. Recall the notes or finger numbers from memory.
7. Write out the bars from memory - don't worry if you can't remember it all, you can always look up what you've forgotten and try again.

Implementing any one or combination of the steps above will help the brain move the information into safer storage. These steps will also help you retain the information for longer, as you are not solely relying on your motor skills. Moreover, they'll slow you down and help you do more thinking and less playing, which inevitably will give you better long-term results.

Practice Methods

At every practice session, you will want to focus on one phrase from your piece. Once you can play the rhythm on one note, and you've *'kinaesthetically practised'* the finger combinations, you are ready to play the phrase with the correct notes. I'll outline two methods that you can use to do that. Your piece will probably lend itself to one or the other, depending upon what you are trying to learn.

Skeleton Playing

I've said this on many occasions throughout this book; the best way to achieve accuracy and consistency is to focus on the individual elements, rather than attempting to do everything at once. Skeleton practice is a continuation of this. Rather than trying to play every note on every beat, you are going to scale it back. By taking additional rests, it gives the brain thinking time. You are going to start with a basic framework and add in more notes as you gain confidence. Here are a few examples:

From Mozart, Piano Sonata No. 16 K54, first movement, bars 1-2

Start by practising the notes that are on the main beats first

Gradually add in more notes.
Tip- leave a rest before a note change in both hands.

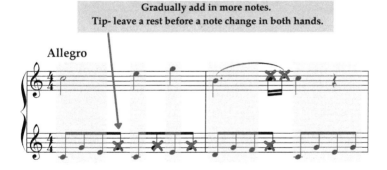

Another example

From Gariboldi, Etudes Mignonnes Op. 131 No 1 bars 45-47

Start with the notes that are on the main beats of the bar

Play the first 3 notes of each grouping

Play the first, third and fourth note of each grouping

179

Build Outwards

Most learners start at bar 1 or the first bar of the phrase they are practicing, but, psychologically, it's often better to start in the middle. When you start in the middle, the phrase can often seem less daunting. You also avoid the possibility of that first bar becoming more accomplished than the other bars.

Start in the middle of the four bars you are practising

From Chopin, Prelude in B Minor, Op.28, No.6, bars 1-3

Take the last beat of bar 2 and the first beat of bar 3, and practice until you can play these notes with ease slowly. Remember, with each repetition, you are aiming to improve, and remember to *always* use a metronome to ensure rhythmic precision. Think about your posture, the tone quality, the articulation and the dynamic level. Engage fully in your practice and listen with care. Then, add a beat on either side of these notes. Again, repeat them using a metronome until you can play them with confidence.

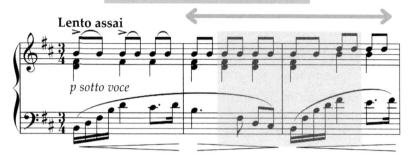

Continue in this way, adding one beat on either side of the notes you are practicing, until you can play the entire phrase, slowly, with a metronome. Now it's time to move on to some blocked practice to strengthen the neural pathways further.

Blocked Practice

Most people repeat things until they make noticeable improvements during their practice sessions. Repeating the action is the way we acquire most skills in life.

Blocked practice means repeating the same thing over and over. The aim is to improve consistency and accuracy to an acceptable level, before moving on to the next task. We all like to practice in this way because we experience noticeable improvements. Hence, we assume that we are making progress. However, the results of blocked practice are often short-lived. I'm sure you've had that experience whereby you've made great strides forward in one session, but the following practice, those improvements seemed to have diminished. That's not such a great feeling.

Blocked practice does have a place, though, especially during your first few practice sessions when learning a new piece. By repeating small sections of music, accurately, every time, you are developing and strengthening the neural pathways. You may recall back in the chapter on how the brain works, that to myelinate a pathway and make an action easy to do, you need to repeat that movement *accurately.*

> **The key element of blocked practice is to ensure EVERY repeat is correct, and accuracy is achieved many times in consecutive attempts.**

You need to remain completely focused, as any errors will strengthen the pathway to your Error file.

Taking my approach of slow practice first, follow my methods to gain rhythmical accuracy. Then you can go through the notes, kinaesthetically. After this, use skeleton playing, or 'build it outwards' to play the bars with the correct notes. This will go a long way to ensure your attempts are accurate.

Blocked practice is not the most effective way to continue, once you have gained some myelination of the neural pathways. Blocked practice methods lull you into a false sense of security because you get results quickly. Remember, adults often judge things by results, so this method is appealling. However, repetition in this way is superficial. Improvements are only stored in the brain's short term memory. Learning is about the process of acquiring knowledge or skill. Therefore, learning should be focused on retention and consistent progress.

You get great satisfaction and **joy** when you've been practising a piece for a while, and you **finally nail that one bar** you've been struggling with. It's taken you so many repetitions to get there, but boy, does it feel good! You want to celebrate, but **what do you do next?** Should you repeat it, and if so, how many times? Or is it OK to move on now?

So often, people move on because they think they can now play it. They think they've got it. They don't need to do that anymore. Unfortunately, it doesn't work like that. *When you play something correctly after many failed attempts, the chances of you getting accurate again are, at best, 50%.*

How should you use blocked practice methods?

Initially, in your first few practice sessions, you need to repeat the bars enough times, accurately, in a row to allow the myelination process to begin.

Points to note

1. To avoid creating error pathways, you should always stop as soon as you make an error. Don't be tempted to go on thinking you'll come back to that mistake in a minute; stop immediately.

2. Talk yourself through the error. What did you do wrong? Why did that happen? What do you need to do to prevent it from happening again? Maybe, you need to focus on the stretch between the fingers or the finger coordination. Take

the two notes out where the error occurred, and go over them many times. When doing this, remain totally focused and committed to correcting that error.

From Bizet, L' Alésienne, 1st Suite, movement 1, Andante molto , bars 2-4

Describe   The finger combination you inaccurately used.

Prescribe   The finger combination you need to use.

Administer   Practice changing from a C to a B natural.

In fact, ironing, is a great analogy to use here. When you have a crease in a shirt, you go over just that area. You may use water, steam or starch to help smooth out the crease. You wouldn't iron the whole shirt again. It's the same when you practice; you need to focus on the error, not the entire phrase.

As a guideline, repeat the phrase, accurately, ten times IN A ROW. That means if you make a mistake on any attempt, you have to go back to one. So let's say you accurately repeat the bar 5 times and on the sixth attempt, you make an error, your next practice attempt is 1. *It can be frustrating, I totally get it, but the process doesn't work if you cheat.* Why? Because as soon as you make a mistake, the brain brings that error pathway back to the fore.

Take regular breaks to help you remain focused, and check off your accurate attempts in your practice diary. In many ways, getting a new piece off the ground is the most challenging part of learning anything. It requires patience and discipline. Avoiding errors, by breaking down the elements before you start the repetitions, helps enormously.

Ideally, you will want to take four bars, and get to 10 accurate repetitions in a row, at a slow tempo each day within your two practice sessions. On day 2, recap these bars once, slowly, and then start work on the next 4 bars. Once you have 3 four-bar sections or phrases that you can play slowly, you'll be ready to include some serial practice, which I'll get onto in the next chapter.

Chapter 13 - Serial Practice

While blocked practice allows you to see improvements during your practice sessions, it doesn't help your retention rate. So, if you are aiming to improve consistently, scientific research has shown that you have to activate the part of the brain that controls higher-order thinking.

When you randomly practice bars, it makes the brain work much harder. The good news is, when it comes to performance, if you practised using serial and random practice methods (which I'll come to shortly), your brain will hardly need to exert much effort to play accurately.

In contrast, if you only use blocked repetition, your brain has to work extremely hard when you perform. Blocked practice methods only strengthen your motor skills, which some people call *'muscle memory.'* Relying on muscle memory for accuracy under pressure gives variable results. Given that you have to deal with other factors such as anxiety and nerves when you perform, I'm sure you'll agree that you'd rather the brain was doing as little work as possible to recall and deliver the music.

Serial practice is a stepping stone towards random practice. Once you have a few phrases that you have practised using blocked practice, you are then going to make the brain work a bit harder, by putting these sections into a series and alternating them in your practice.

For example, you'll practice bars 1-4 for two minutes, then you'll switch to bars 13-16 for two minutes, and then switch to bars 5-8 for two minutes. You'll then go back to bars 1-4 and repeat the process. The aim is to play each 4 bar phrase accurately 5 times in a row. Remember, if you make an error, you lose all your accurate repetitions and will need to start again. At first, you may find this method of practice challenging and at times frustrating. There will be a temptation to resort to blocked practice, but I urge you to resist. By switching bars frequently, you are likely to make mistakes at first, but as your level of focus develops, so will the level of accuracy.

Serial Practice

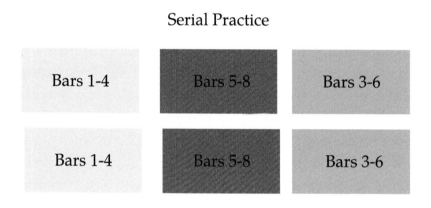

You will find that with some phrases, you'll have no problem getting to five accurate repetitions. If this is the case, you can stop practising those bars for now. However, within other phrases, you'll find that you struggle to get 5 accurate repetitions in a row. If you are making different mistakes each time, it's your lack of focus that's the problem. Take a break, do some mindful practice, which I'll come to shortly, and try again in your second practice of the day.

If the mistake you are making happens at the same place each time, you need to go back and do some more blocked practice on that bar. Maybe, you are messing up a shift in the hand position, or the rhythm isn't accurate, in which case you need to go back to doing 10 accurate repetitions, slowly in a row. Then, perhaps, gradually build that bar up with a metronome to strengthen the neural pathway.

You can keep working on new phrases, using blocked practice, and adding them to your serial practice when they are ready.

I like to use a traffic light system on my music to help me see which phrases are secure, in which case I leave them to one side (green, ready to go), which phrases I am practicing using serial practice (amber, in preparation), and which bars I have still to practise (red, not yet started or still in blocked practice mode).

From Bach (Christian Petzold), Notebook for Anna Magdalena,
Minuet in G Major, BWV Anh 114, bars 1-16

As more and more bars become secure, you can then move on
to random practice and increase the tempo gradually.

Random Practice

We all want to play with a high degree of accuracy when we
perform, and the best way to achieve this is through random
practice. Random practice is challenging, as it relies on your
brain pulling out the *correct file* quickly. It doesn't quite work
like that, but I think it's an excellent way to imagine how the

brain stores information. Think of a phrase, and everything that needs to happen for you to play that phrase accurately. So, this will include: the finger combinations, the rhythms, the articulation, the intonation, the musical idea etc., and then, imagine that this information is stored in a file. Each phrase has its own file, but in many ways, they are similar. Random practice allows the brain to practice the cognitive shifts required to access the correct information, in other words to pull out the correct files.

There are various ways that you can use random practice and, as you develop your practice methods, you can get more creative.

To begin, write the bar numbers of your phrases on separate pieces of paper and, put them in a bag. Pull out a piece of paper, and play the bars once as if you were performing. In other words, if you make a mistake, don't stop. Then pull out the next phrase, and perform that one. Go through all your phrases, and then start the process again. If you find that you are making different mistakes, your level of focus isn't quite there yet. However, if you make the same mistake, you'll need to do more blocked practice on that error.

At this stage, you can begin preparing to learn a new piece. You'll recall, I said previously that spaced learning helps the brain move the information into long term storage. Take a few days off from practising this piece, and begin work on something new. Then, allocate a practice session several days later to some further random practice on the old piece. Remember to document your progress at the end of each practice session. A fun way to incorporate random practice while working on new material is with an *interval timer*. You can set it to go off at a specific time. When it does, you have to pull a piece of paper, containing your phrase, out of your bag, and perform those few bars.

Mental Practice

Few things in life are as powerful as mental practice. It's like a magician whose illusions seem so real that you begin to doubt that magic is just a trick. Yet you know there's no such thing as magic, right? However, what if I was to tell you that there is no magic involved in mental practice? The effects are real, not illusionary. When mental practice is done correctly, it has the power to *change the brain.* For learners, that's another complex concept to grasp, and one which is often dismissed. You see, like everything else with the learning process, if you judge yourself by the end result, having done little practice on the technique, you will be disappointed.

The ability to practise mentally is what often separates the great from the good. In the world of golf, there is no better champion of the mental game than Tiger Woods. He practised every shot mentally, both on and off the green. It's become the norm, amongst the world's leading sportspeople, that mentally rehearsing their strokes, the game, and their own emotions is all part of becoming a success.

191

It's not only sportspeople who use mental practice to get ahead. Musicians such as Rubenstein, Horowitz and Gleseking were all supporters of mental practice. There is an overwhelming amount of research which shows mental practice works. The world of science now has the scanners and data to prove that when you mentally practise something in a multi-sensory way, the same neurological changes happen - to almost the same extent - as they would if you were to practise physically.

Mental practice produces fundamental changes and genuine improvements. However, it's a skill that you need to practise. Mental practice is not the same as imagining yourself playing the notes, reading through the score, or picturing the notes. It has to involve all of your senses. You have to mentally *visualise* how it feels and sounds when you play those notes. You have to think about the notes, the rhythm, the articulation, the phrase shapes, the muscle movements, your environment, your posture, how the keys or strings feel to touch and how each note sounds. Hence, it's no wonder that, as a learner, you are yet to experience the true benefits that mental practice has to offer.

Most of us are no stranger to daydreaming, and many of us will have indulged in imaginary play as children. Any time you go through the motions of something inside your head, you are mentally practising. To reap the benefits on your instrument, you have to incorporate regular mental practice into your practice regime. Dedicate 10-15 minutes of mental practice daily, and you will notice the difference when you physically practise.

While mental practise is no replacement for physical practice, it is a fantastic way to make progress when you cannot get to your instrument. Mental practice also has another benefit: it increases your memory retention and your performance delivery.

So how do you get started?
Start by sitting somewhere comfortable and closing your eyes. Focus on your breathing, and then start to release any tension in the body. Relax the shoulders, jaw, facial muscles, arms, back, hips, legs, knees, and toes. If you practise yoga, pilates or tai chi etc., you'll be familiar with this type of exercise. You'll recall in Chapter 7 on posture, I said that lying in the semi supine position is a great way to practise visualisation. Let all the tension melt away, and be content to sit in a completely relaxed state.

See if you can visualise your practice space. Does it have a window? If so, how do the curtains or blinds hang in the window? What furniture is in the room? Are there any cushions or throws? Where is your instrument in the room? What music is on your music stand? Where is your metronome? Is there a pencil nearby? Imagine as much detail as you can. Then think about what you can hear when you are in the room. Perhaps if the room is next to a road, you can hear the cars passing? Maybe you can hear another family member watching television in a room close by? It could be that you can hear the air-conditioning whirring away, or the electricity buzzing. Imagine what the room smells like. Perhaps you have a scented air freshener, or you can smell food being prepared as you always practise at dinner time.

Go through this exercise over several days, and see if you can recall more details about your practice space.

When you feel that you know your practice space intimately, and can easily visualise it, try the following:

- Visualise yourself practising a scale.
- How are you sitting or standing?
- Can you identify any areas of concern in your posture?
- What does your hand position look like?
- Do you need to correct it?
- What is your breathing like?
- What do the keys or strings feel like under your fingers?
- Can you hear the notes of the scale as you play them?
- What is your tone like?
- What do your muscles feel like as you change the finger combinations?
- Mentally recall all the sensory movements and sounds involved in playing that scale on your instrument in as much detail as you can.

Mentally practice playing that scale, and make improvements where necessary. Maybe you can feel how awkward it is to change between certain finger combinations, or you can see that your posture isn't right. If you can visualise yourself hesitating before a note, mentally practice that change. For the best results, you will want to do mental practice without moving any part of the body. However, you may first need to mime the finger movements or look over the notes. If you are finding this challenging, start by mentally practising only the first few notes.

As your visualisation skills develop, you'll want to practise, mentally, small sections of your piece. See yourself playing the notes, and hear the pitches in your head. Recall the articulation and performance detail. Mentally practise the phrasing, breathing, vibrato, the pedalling, your musical intentions and, basically, everything that's involved in playing that section exquisitely.

It takes time to become adept at mental practice. In many ways, it's harder than physically practising, but the benefits are worth the hours of patience and dedication. Those who regularly engage in the power of mental practice, are far more likely to make better and more consistent progress.

Chapter 14 - How to Structure Your Practice

I have covered a lot so far in this book, and I know that many learners like to have a structure to follow. While I wish there were a clear template that I could provide, there isn't one! It depends on what level you are at, what challenges you are facing, what problems you need to address and much more. However, there are guidelines that you can follow and adapt when necessary.

Whatever level you are at, you want to take a holistic approach to learning. Gradually developing your technique, rhythmic skills, sight-reading ability, mindset, practice methods, and awareness alongside each other - will help you make consistent progress. Until you've built solid foundations, keep things simple by focusing on one piece of music that you can learn in one week.

Practice Session Overview

1. Read practice diary and warm-up
2. Scale/ arpeggio warm-up
3. 2nd warm-up eg chords, large leaps
4. Practice small section of piece
5. Further scale/ arpeggio warm-up
6. Practice section of piece with a different focus
7. Have fun playing pieces that you can already play
8. Recap once everything you have practiced
9. Reflect in your practice book

To help you understand better how to implement this structure, here's an example of a practice plan to follow for the piece below.

Sunday. Highlight the music and plan practice routine. Find a good recording to listen to and do some research on the composer.

Coloured boxes show bars that repeat

* Day 1 Yo yo exercise

From A. Reinagle, 24 Short and Easy pieces, No.4

Monday. Listen to the piece after breakfast. Do the simple 5 note exercise using the notes CDEFG in the right hand. Warm-up two: use Yo-Yo exercise using the notes D-F and then E-G. Practise bars 1-4. Say, clap and play, on one note, the rhythm with a metronome at 60. Read through the letter names, and kinaesthetically practice. Do 5 note exercise with the left hand. Use the *build it outwards* method. Visualise the right notes throughout the day, and see if you can recall them from memory. Aim to do 10 accurate repetitions of bars 1-4, using a metronome.

Monday Bars 1-4

Yo Yo warm up exercise

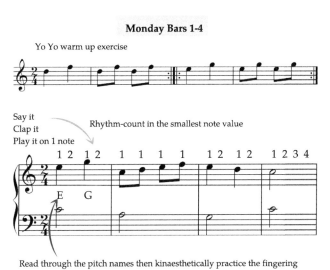

Read through the pitch names then kinaesthetically practice the fingering

Build outwards from bar 2

198

Tuesday. Simple 5 note exercise using the notes CDEFG. Practise these softly. 2nd warm-up - create 'hands together' exercise. Focus on bars 5-8. Say, clap and play rhythm on one note. Read through the letter names and kinaesthetically practise the fingers. Use the Skeleton method to put the bars together. Mentally practise bars 1-4, then practice bars 1-4, while gradually increasing the speed with the metronome. Try and recall the notes of bars 5-8 throughout the day. Listen to the piece while cooking dinner.

Tuesday bars 5-8

Chord warm up bars 5-8, the first note in each hand

Wednesday. C major scale warm-up, followed by chord exercise from bars 9-10. Say, clap and play the rhythm on one note of bars 9-14. Kinaesthetically, practise the letter names and fingers. Use the 'build out method' to put the bars together. Work on the dynamics of bars 15-16. Recap bars 1-4 slowly at 60 on the metronome.

Wednesday bars 9-14

Practice hands separately the diminuendo in bars 15-16- make each note softer

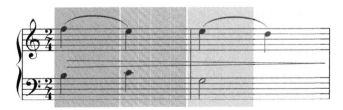

Thursday. C Major scale warm-up. Practice right hand of bars 9 and 14 with dynamics. Put these two bars together by yo-yoing between the notes. Start serial practice at 2 minute intervals, of bars 1-4 9-14 then 5-8. Aim to do 10 accurate repetitions of each, and do some more blocked practice, if necessary. Listen to the piece and visualise playing the notes.

Thursday -serial practice

C major scale warm up

warm up 2- Practice the right hand of bars 9-14 with dynamics

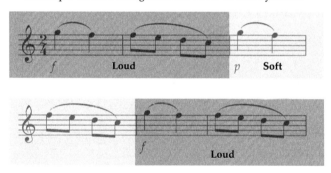

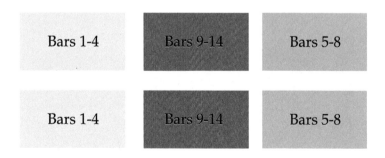

Serial practice switch at 2 minute intervals- aim for 10 accurate repetitions

Bars 1-4	Bars 9-14	Bars 5-8
Bars 1-4	Bars 9-14	Bars 5-8

Friday. C major scale warm-up, using the rhythm of bar 9-10. Serial practice, at 2 minute intervals, bars 1-4, 9-14, 5-8, 15-16. Practice dynamics, and speed up the bars using a metronome.

Friday -Further serial practice

C major scale warm up exercise using rhythms from the piece

Serial practice, switching at 2 minute intervals and gradually increasing the speed.

Bars 1-4	Bars 9-14	Bars 5-8	Bars 15-16
Bars 1-4	Bars 9-14	Bars 5-8	Bars 15-16

Saturday. Choose random phrases to play 3 times: once at 80, 90, 100 with the metronome. Do some blocked practice, if necessary. Play the whole piece through, slowly.

Saturday -Random practice

Bars 5-8	Bars 9-14	Bars 1-4	Bars 15-16
Bars 1-4	Bars 15-16	Bars 5-8	Bars 9-14

Each day you should *reflect* on your progress. It may be necessary to *amend* your schedule if you encounter a challenge with a specific bar, in which case, create an exercise to use in your warm-up to help you solve the problem. You have to *adapt* accordingly throughout the process.

Adaptive learning involves a combination of blocked, serial and random practice. *For the most part, this is an ideal way to practise*, especially if you are more advanced, or you know the piece reasonably well.

You take a section of music and focus on a particular aspect, such as pitch, rhythm or coordination. You repeat the action (each attempt should be accurate), until you start to gain confidence. At this point, you want to increase the difficulty, so maybe you switch to another passage, or you focus on the balance, intonation or dynamics. You can also start serial and random practice methods. By pushing ourselves, we raise our awareness and concentration levels. However, if more errors start to occur and the challenge proves too much, you revert to some more blocked practice.

More advanced players should start with the most challenging parts of the piece. I like to add post-it notes alongside those bars and check off the number of accurate repetitions.

If you are playing more challenging works, your rhythmic skills and sight-reading should be further developed. Hence, you shouldn't need to clap out the rhythms of every bar. You'll also be more adept at knowing what your strengths and weaknesses are, and can, therefore, tailor your practice sessions towards resolving those weaknesses.

Section 4

Perceive and Conquer

Chapter 15 - Problems and Solutions

As you make progress along your musical journey, you'll continually develop and refine your practice methods. You'll become more aware of your strengths and weaknesses. There will be times when your mindset needs attention, or you come up against hurdles in your practice which you struggle to overcome. There are always obstacles and challenges that we need to navigate. In this section of the book, I'll cover some ideas to help you keep moving forward.

Your Strengths and Weaknesses

We all have strengths and weaknesses, both personally and musically. As a recovering perfectionist, I know that I can be overly self-critical if I'm trying to accomplish something. For most people, fear is the real problem that lurks beneath perfectionism. Whether that be fear of failure, of getting it wrong or something else. Perfectionism is Procrastination's twin sister: where one is, the other will not be far behind, they often appear together.

You have to learn to accept that nothing is perfect; you can continually improve upon everything. You can only do your best. It's finding the balance between the time you have, the money available and the level of personal investment you can commit to.

These days, I reframe perfectionism as 'perfect in the time frame available.' I thought that resonated with lots of things in music. Take sight-reading, for example. So many people tell me that their sight-reading is terrible. The number one problem is that they stop as soon as they make a mistake. As adults, it's hard to keep going when we've made a mistake. It's essential to remember that you can't expect things to be close to perfection if you are sight-reading a piece for the first time. You can, however, expect to sight-read a piece as perfectly as is possible, in the time frame available.

So many people have asked me if I can help them to improve their sight-reading? And the answer is YES! When you can sight-read music, it opens the flood gates to much more music. It makes learning new repertoire much more fun, and you'll make much more progress in less time. It's essential to understand the close connection between the way you practise and your ability to sight-read. By learning one new piece per week, and implementing the methods shared in this book, you are developing your sight reading skills.

Why do people find sight reading so tricky?
Sight reading tests all of your musical skills. It's a culmination of basically, everything there is in music. You've got to be able to feel the pulse, not just with a metronome, but also internally, and you've got to be able to keep that beat steady throughout the music.

Secondly, you've got to be able to count the rhythms, and you've got to be able to absorb information quickly. You also need the ability to read the notes, work out what key the piece is in and it helps if you can recognise chord progressions, phrasing in music and cadence points.

Then we've got to decode the music.
- You've got to decipher all that information going on in your head.
- You need to learn to read ahead, be prepared for the unfamiliar, because you are sight reading.
- You've got to be able to recognise patterns.
- You've got to be able to hear the music, internally, and on top of that, you've got to feel confident.

So, when you put all that together, is it any wonder that we find sight reading a challenge? I don't think so!

The best way to improve your sight reading is to start looking at each of those individual elements. Does this sound familiar? I hope so, as throughout this book I have talked on numerous occasions about the importance of building strong musical foundations.

Here are a few more tips that will improve your sight-reading and help you make better progress.

Read notes like you read words: that means quickly!
Our eyes operate like a camera and, if we have learnt the vocabulary, we can sight-read words even if they are presented distorted, written backwards, or have had all their vowels removed. You need to become familiar with reading notes as you are with letters.

On instruments such as the harp or piano, sight reading is more challenging as there are two lines of music to read. Most people are confident with the treble clef notes; however, they need to improve their bass clef sight reading.

How can you improve your note reading?

There is no quick way to improve sight reading music notes; you've got to practice repetitively. Here are a few suggestions to help.

• Make yourself some note cards, and practice naming notes regularly, every day. As you progress include accidental signs and ledger lines. You can also make some cards showing chords, intervals or cadences, to develop your skills further. If you don't mind spending a little money, purchase an app to help you such as Treble Cat, Bass cat or Note Rush.

• Find some note-naming exercises and practice them regularly. If you type 'note naming exercises' into google, you'll find plenty of examples.

• Spell out words on manuscript paper. See the examples below:

ACE	FED	BED	AGE
FAB	BEG	DAD	BAD
EGG	BAG	CAFE	DEAF
FACE	BEEF	FADE	CAGE
DEAD	AGED	BADGE	ADDED
FACADE	DECADE	BAGGAGE	CABBAGE

• Read through the pitch names of any piece of music, don't forget to check the key signature and include the accidentals when you read through the notes.

Orientation Sight Reading Game

In addition to reading the notes quickly, you also have to be able to find the notes on your instrument. Spacial awareness is equally as important. A fun way to practise this is by playing the words you can make from the letters A B C D E F G. Make yourself a list or use the one above!

You can develop the activity by mixing the octaves, range and key. You can also make it more fun by setting a timer and seeing how many words you can play in one minute.

Read Ahead Sight-Reading Practice.

Being able to read ahead is a crucial skill, when it comes to improving your sight-reading skills and your ability to play music fluently. It's one of the hardest things to practise, and developing your memory skills is essential.

There are some video read ahead exercises available in the additional resources for this book.

Learn to absorb as much information about the music, before you begin playing. Take a brief look at the piece of music on the following page and then answer the questions below it.

Andante [♩=80]

- What is the time signature?
- What is the key signature?
- Is the first note G or D?
- Can you clap the rhythm of the first phrase?
- What dynamic marking is at the start of the piece?
- What is the metronome mark?

Quick study tests, such as the one above, are fantastic exercises to do in your lunch hour, or while you are waiting for the kids, or standing in line at the supermarket. Take pictures of your music, so that you have them to hand on your phone, for such occasions.

Apologies, that was a rather large deviation from discussing those character traits that can sometimes hold us back. Another 'thought-intruder' that often likes to interfere with our progress, is 'imposter syndrome.' Like perfectionism and procrastination, imposter syndrome is triggered by anxiety. We seek approval from others throughout most of our lives, whether that be from parents or from our superiors in the workplace. We do our utmost to conform, and our actions are usually motivated by the desire for acceptance, or maximum approval, from others. We all love to hear that we have performed a particular task fantastically well. Yet, being told that you are fantastic at something implies that others are, shall we say, not so fantastic. There usually comes a time when the latter applies to yourself, and that's when self-doubt begins to establish itself. These thought processes often stem back to childhood, where the first seeds of self-doubt are sown. Many more people than you think, especially high flyers and achievers, suffer from imposter syndrome.

Self-doubt turns into beliefs such as - I'm faking it, or I just got lucky. You find it difficult to take compliments or to celebrate your achievements, no matter how significant they might be. You may have experienced this yourself after a performance or music lesson when someone has congratulated you, and instead of feeling delighted, you're thinking about those things that you got wrong. Seeking perfection often leads to procrastination and can sometimes lead to imposter syndrome, but the good news is: all three are behavioural responses to a situation, and you can learn to overcome them. It's not an easy journey, and for many, you will probably need some professional guidance, but it is totally possible to change your response to habits of behaviour. I'm not a psychologist, but below are a few suggestions to help you get started.

1. Lower your expectations

Learning to play a musical instrument is challenging, and it's unlikely that you'll ever deliver the perfect version that you hear inside of you. Even the best musicians in the world have things they'd love to change about every performance. See your mistakes as opportunities to learn rather than as signs of failure.

2. Learn to rephrase things

During my years of teaching in education, and through my experiences as an examiner, I've become attuned to the idea of turning negative statements into positive ones. I remember finding my first attempts at writing school reports so challenging back in 1999. My thought processes back then were rather one-dimensional, and my perfectionist traits were very much to the fore. Since then, I've spent years developing my mindset, and now find that rephrasing negative statements comes much more easily. Instead of saying to yourself - that was terrible, I made loads of mistakes, try rephrasing it to *I need to make improvements the next time I play.* As a general rule, avoid using negatives and employ active verbs (in the feedback to yourself) when you self-evaluate.

3. Learn to recognise the triggers early

Stress has a habit of escalating fast; however, you can make changes if you can identify the early signs and address them. For example, if you are frustrated in your practice, take a break. When you return, think about the cause of that frustration and how you can overcome the problem.

4. Develop new habits

Ask yourself what your values are, and establish new habits that will support your learning. Focus on your achievements, and resist the temptation to compare yourself to others. Comparing yourself to a professional musician who's probably done thousands of hours more practice than you, for example, is a pitfall for feeling like you don't measure up. Stop putting others around you on a pedestal. Take note of your achievements, and when you receive compliments, accept them gracefully, put them in a safe folder and refer to them regularly.

5. Talk to someone

There's a well-known proverb that says a problem shared is a problem halved. By sharing your experiences with a teacher or friend, you are more likely to realise that feelings of being an imposter are not uncommon. They might also help you see the irrationalities in your thoughts and give you ideas on moving forward.

6. Separate feelings from the truth

Be mindful of any feelings that could be an early warning of imposter syndrome creeping in. What we feel about ourselves and the objective reality are often two entirely different things. If you can hear the voice inside your head saying things such as: I'm not making progress, remind yourself that you are capable of learning and will almost certainly know more than you want to admit to. Make a list of everything you have achieved, and celebrate your successes.

The truth is, learning to play an instrument is a lifelong journey. There will always be more accomplished people than you, so forget about being competitive, and enjoy the learning process. Music has so much to offer - so open the door to your mind and let your passion flourish.

Another question I am frequently asked is, 'How can I play faster?'

Learners can often play music accurately slowly, but they make mistakes as they go faster. There are multiple reasons why you struggle to play quicker, but most are linked either to

1. Tension in the body or incorrect posture

2. Insufficient practice in a variety of ways.

Often the two are connected because if you can't play the notes with ease, you will most likely be holding tension in your body.

How to gain ease control and precision with faster passage-work.

Repeating a passage of semiquavers with a metronome will likely gain you some control and precision, but it may not be enough to nail those notes accurately every time. Here are a few other ideas to try:

- Practice the passage with different rhythms as shown below and on the next page.

Vivo

Glazunov Saxophone Concert, Op. 109, excert from the cadenza

- Practice the passage with additional rests, in a similar way to the skeleton method I described

- Yo-Yo, practice between notes that you find difficult to coordinate. Remember to focus on the finger that's moving too slowly.
- Practice the passage accenting different notes
- Memorise the notes: you can do this by mental practice, writing the notes out and verbalising them.
- Practice the passage with different articulation patterns.
- Work backwards with a metronome. This method requires a lot of focus, and often you'll find that you make more mistakes the slower you go. Start at a tempo that is at the cusp of your ability, and then work backwards in increments of 10 until you get to a super slow speed, such as 40 crotchet beats per minute. You are aiming to get the passage correct on your first attempt. Notice where you have a tendency to rush as you slow the passage right down. Sometimes, it's a mindset thing. We think we can't play it fast, but in reality, we are still struggling to control it when playing slowly. Other times, the level of focus that you experience, when playing super slow, allows you to let go when you try it at a much faster tempo, and the results can often take you by surprise. You'll find, that you can play it fast and accurately; you just didn't believe that you could.

Improving Coordination

Flaws in our coordination can often mean that we need more practice. Sometimes, they are due to lack of focus, sometimes they are due to weakness in the finger. There are a number of exercises that you can do to strengthen your coordination.

- Try drawing a circle with one hand while simultaneously, drawing a triangle with the other hand. This is a fun exercise and one that requires a lot of concentration and hand independence.
- Play a repeated pattern (ostinato) with one hand on your instrument and try doing an action with the other hand. You could open a book, for example, or write your name on a piece of paper.

The ostinato pattern that you are playing should stay in time while you do the action. When I do this with my students, I ask them questions, and they have to answer, without compromising the evenness and flow of the ostinato pattern.

Finger Isolation Exercises

Place your hand on a flat surface, with your fingers naturally curved. See if you can lift your thumb up and down to make a tapping noise. Repeat for each of your fingers, making sure that only the finger you are moving lifts away from the flat surface.

You can develop this exercise by lifting your outer fingers up and down, simultaneously, or by using various combinations of your fingers and thumb. Aim to lift and lower them at the same time, so you only get one tapping noise on the flat surface.

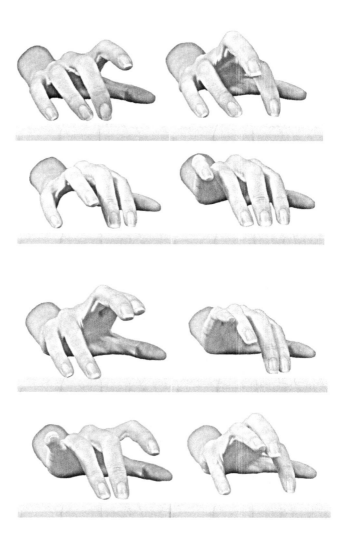

To make the exercise even more challenging, use both hands and different combinations of fingers. The aim is still to get one tapping noise on your flat surface.

Separate the Fingers- Exercise

Again, this is an exercise that requires independent finger isolation and a lot of focus. Hold your hand in a relaxed position. Hold fingers 1 and 2 together, so they are touching, and fingers 3 and 4 together, so they are also touching. Now see if you can widen the gap between fingers 2 and 3, without the other finger combinations separating.

You can develop this by holding fingers 2 and 3 together and separating fingers 1 and 4 out. Try alternating the two patterns. Hold fingers 1, 2, 3 together, while opening and closing your little finger. Then hold fingers 2, 3 and 4 together, while opening out your first finger.

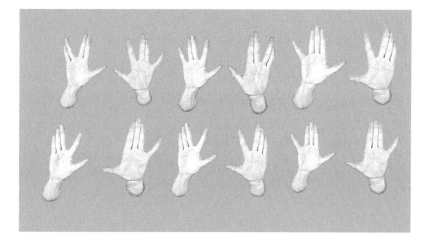

Challenge yourself further by doing different patterns with both hands, simultaneously. These types of hand exercises are great as you can do them anytime, anywhere.

Rhythmic Coordination Exercises

Metronomes are fantastic at helping us maintain a steady beat, but we still have to be able to coordinate our notes with the click, which isn't easy. Below are some exercises to help.

- Vocalise the counts while clapping a steady, crotchet beat, pulse.
- Clap the rhythm of the melody while marching on the spot, in time to the beat.
- Tap the rhythm of the phrase with one hand, and tap the beat with the other hand.

- Tap the rhythm of one phrase with one hand and the rhythm of another phrase with the other hand.

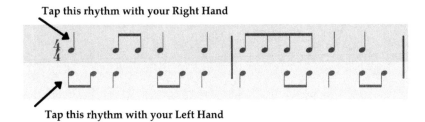

- Stand on one leg, and clap the rhythm to a metronome. You may think that this sounds silly, and to some extent it is, but you will need to focus on your balance as well as on the rhythm, which is more challenging than you think.

Intonation

If you have one particular note in a bar that is out of tune, start at the beginning of the phrase, and stop on that note. Discern whether the note is too high or too low. Now, without correcting the note, ask yourself what you need to adjust, for that note to sound in the *middle* of its *tonal centre*. You may need to move the finger slightly on the fret or increase the air support on a wind instrument. Start the phrase again; this time, be aware of the change you need to make and stop again on the note. Once you are able to hit the note with the correct intonation, repeat until you can do it, accurately, at least 5 times in a row.

Below I've outlined two exercises which you can use to develop your intonation and inner ear.

1. Record yourself playing the first 6 notes of a scale, both ascending and descending slowly. Now play the first 5 notes of the scale up and down, to your recording. If you play the piano, you could use your voice to develop your inner ear. When you sing or play along to your recording, you'll be in unison on the way up and in 3rds on the way down—a brilliant way to get better at intonation. You can extend the exercise to a full octave; just record the first octave plus one note.

Record yourself playing the exercise below

Now play the following to your recording

Result- playing or singing in 3rds with yourself descending

2. Practice your piece to a drone. Pick the key note of the piece, or the note that occurs the most frequently in the phrase, and record it as a long note. Use a tuning machine if necessary to check the tuning. With practice, you will be able to hear if there are any intonation flaws in the melody.

From Bach, Notebook for Anna Magdalena, Musette, BWV Anh 126, bars 1-4

Most common note-A

Key note- D

Improving the Textural Balance.

One of the biggest challenges for multi-lined instruments is balance. You always want the melody to be brought to the fore, which can be easier said than done! To develop hand independence and balance here are a few suggestions.

1. Mime the left hand while playing the right hand and vice versa.

2. Play the melody, and add only the bass notes that are played on the downbeat. Gradually, add in the other main beats and then any further subdivisions.

From Mendelssohn, Songs without words Op. 19, No.6, bars 3-5

3. Play the bass notes, staccato, and the melody with the correct articulation and vice versa.

4. Sing the melody, while playing only the bass and harmony lines.

5. Record the melody and practise the bass/ harmony parts along to your recording, so you can hear the balance that you are trying to achieve.

Chapter 16 - Focus and Awareness

Music practice can often reap excellent results one day and inconsistent ones the next. The likelihood is that your bad habits will thrive regardless. Bad habits are like the weeds in your garden: they are persistent and grow, come rain or shine. Thankfully, we have more control over our music practice, and we can make changes that will get us results.

Often, as adults, we judge things by our achievements, in other words, the musical outcomes of our playing. However, a more effective way to make progress is to focus more on our awareness.

Taking a step back to look at the bigger picture is something I highly recommend with your music practice. Often, learners do the same old thing each practice, which can lead to frustration or lack of motivation.

Have you ever been frustrated while practising? Perhaps you've been over a bar a few times, slowly, but you can't get it up to speed. What do you do? Do you keep going over it, still getting it wrong past a certain speed, and getting more and more frustrated? Then, you do something else and repeat the whole process the next time you practise, hoping that things will improve. Or **do you stop** and take a look from the outside in, and **identify the actual problem?**

I've had tuition from numerous music teachers, and one of the most important lessons I learnt was from Richard Ingham. Richard is a phenomenal saxophonist/composer/educator and author of the The Cambridge Companion to the Saxophone. He once said to me:

"It doesn't matter how many times you practice that bar, Fiona. You're never going to be able to play it ..."

As you can imagine, at that point in my lesson, I was on the verge of bursting into tears and about to give up on my dream of being a musician.
He then added:

"... your wrist is too high when hitting the left-hand palm key".

I went away and practised some exercises, keeping this specific criticism in mind, and - BINGO - I could play that passage within a couple of days.

It makes sense, doesn't it? If you identify the real problem, you can find a solution and make progress. I like to think of it as 'mindful practice'. You are more capable than you might think of identifying problems, once you start thinking in this way. Golf players, tennis masters, Olympic swimmers, baseball players and countless other sports people use video analysis to pinpoint errors, identify areas for improvement, and maximise performance.

Most of us have access to recording equipment on our phones and tablets, so why not use it? Yes, it takes a bit of effort to set up. However, it's worth it, and it will save you a lot of time in the long run. When we are practising, we often focus on one thing: the rhythm, breathing or speed, to name but a few, so we don't honestly evaluate our playing as a whole.

So Take Action!
Record yourself practising, then watch the video back - ideally in slow motion. Even if you can't watch it in slow motion, the exercise is still worth doing. Observe your posture, and see if there are any areas you could improve? Listen and check the accuracy of the notes and rhythm. Question the musicality in your playing and think about how you could improve the delivery of your musical intentions.

There's a lot to do when we play a piece of music, regardless of whether you read music or play by ear. You've got to coordinate the fingers, keep a beat, play rhythmically and fluently. If you attempt to do everything simultaneously, that's when your awareness suffers.

So what can you do?

Follow what you've learnt so far in this book.
Take a bite-size section of music, and before you practice.

- **Vocalise the rhythm:** A quick tip here, avoid subdivision. Instead, count in the smallest note value.

- **Clap out the rhythm:** You'll get a good idea of what the rhythm sounds like by doing this.
- **Play the rhythm on one note.**
- **Read through the letter names.**

Before you put everything together, play the section of music, silently. When we mime the actions before we play, it prepares the body and mind for accuracy. Then, try playing a few bars, slowly, using either 'skeleton playing' or 'build out' method.

At every step of this process, raise your awareness. If you make a mistake, see if you can recall what the error was. Perhaps, you used an incorrect finger, or you held a note for two beats instead of one. By telling yourself this, rather than saying the rhythm was wrong, you'll be much more aware on your next attempt. When you take this approach, you'll see that progress is much more rewarding and consistent. This is one thing that professional musicians do, that learners don't. It makes the outcome of their practice sessions more successful. When they make a mistake, they describe their error in a specific way that's related to the cause. If you've ever listened to interviews with sportspeople, you'll have noticed many of them do the same thing: they identify a specific problem as, for example, in the following statement - *'I didn't extend my neck fully coming out of the final turn.'* In doing this, they are allowing themselves to have a more specific goal on the next attempt.

Learners, on the other hand, **tend to reflect in a more general way.**

They say things like *'my rhythm was off,'* or *'I played it wrong.'* These sorts of responses are not specific, nor do they highlight the cause of the problem, so they do little to help you improve on your next practice attempt. So how should you talk to yourself when you make a mistake, or a practice attempt didn't go the way you wanted?

Here are a few suggestions:

Instead of saying the rhythm was wrong - describe exactly which note you held for too long or not long enough:

'I played the B in the right hand as a quaver (eighth note) instead of a crotchet (quarter note).'

Rather than say the notes were inaccurate - be specific: what note did you play and what note should you have played.

'I played an F natural on the fourth beat of bar 3, and it should have been an F sharp.'

Instead of saying there were gaps in that bar - ask yourself what caused them.

'I didn't stretch my little finger out when changing chords in the left hand so I was late playing the beat.'

Put your detective hat on, and focus on identifying the exact problem and why it happened. Ask yourself what tweaks and adjustments you can make to get things right on your next attempt. So often, when learners make a mistake, they immediately go right into another practice attempt, without figuring out what went wrong and why the last one didn't go correctly. During your next practice session, I want to encourage you to describe your errors specifically and include what you need to change on your next attempt. In doing this, you will raise your awareness and get closer to your goals. Then, remember to write down the error and the cause in your practice diary, as this will raise your awareness even further.

Deepening Your Focus.
So often, in music practice, we are faced with distractions. These might be external, like the phone ringing, or from that internal inner voice with which you happen to be having a conversation. These internal conversations frequently distract our attention from what we are trying to focus on. We can, however, accept the distractions and choose to focus our attention elsewhere. We can increase our awareness of the music and lessen the frustration we feel at the distractions.

Here's an exercise to try which is suggested *in The Inner Game of Music* by Barry Green.

As you read this, begin to focus on the sounds that you can hear. Perhaps it's the noise of cars passing, the buzzing of electricity, or, if you are lucky enough to live somewhere warm and sunny, you can hear the air conditioning buzzing away.

Now focus on one of these sounds. Ask yourself:

- Is the noise constant?
- Is the volume steady?
- Does the sound have a rhythm?
- Does the sound have high and low pitches, or is it a continual note?

Stay with the sound for a little longer.

While you were focusing on this sound, did the other sounds around you fade into the background?

Focusing on the sound you make when practising is a great way to reduce other distractions including the internal voice that talks to you. It's also a great way to relax the muscles and release any stress or tension in the body. You'll notice more about how you are playing, which is always beneficial. Revisit that simple exercise I described in Chapter 9 and focus completely - on the sound you make.

Chapter 17 - Stop Making Excuses

'I know I need to practise, but …'

I taught for 20 years in a school setting, so I've heard every excuse under the sun, as to why practice hasn't happened much this week. For the most part, the reasons were nothing more than excuses, but occasionally I heard a tale that was more interesting. A young student, Samantha, once turned up to her lesson with her hand heavily bandaged. I didn't expect the answer I received, though, when I asked what was the matter with her hand. From what I can remember, the tale went something like this:

"I was putting my clarinet away, having done lots of practice, Miss Berry. There was lots of spit in my clarinet, and you always tell us to clean it out before it goes back in the box. So I did, but I put my finger down the mouthpiece and it got it stuck."

"Oh dear," I said, "why would you put your finger down the mouthpiece?"

"To make sure it was dry, I didn't want my favourite reed to go mouldy," replied Samantha.

"But I always tell you to take the reed off, and put it back in its case." As I said this, I thought she must have done that anyway; otherwise, she couldn't have stuck her finger in the mouthpiece."

"I had taken the reed off Miss Berry, but the water ran away, so I was checking to see if it was dry. Anyway, mummy couldn't get my finger out, and in the end, we had to go to the hospital."

"Oh dear!" I said again, "how did they get it off at the hospital?"

"Well, they tried all sorts of things, but in the end, a fireman had to come with his drill. We were at the hospital all night, and my fingers are now very sore. I don't have a mouthpiece anymore because it had to be broken to rescue my finger. So I can't practice."

You'll be delighted to hear that Samantha went on to be a very good clarinetist. I did tell her many years later when she was in 6th form, that I would one day share that story. I always keep my word Sam, and if you ever read this, I hope you are keeping well.

As a music teacher, not finding the time to practise is something I hear frequently from students. I will cut to the chase straight away, and tell you something that you will probably not want to hear. It's a *mindset shift* that you need to make because, wait for it ....

It's not that you don't *have* the time: it's that you don't *make* the time.

We all deserve at least 20 minutes a day to ourselves, and you must carve that time away from your schedule to do just that.

1. Start by making yourself a schedule and sticking to it. Often people who are short of time are those who don't budget their time, or plan ahead. Analyse the actual time you need to do each activity in your day and stick to it.
2. Don't multitask when it comes to your music practice - limit yourself to learning one piece at a time. Plan, your sessions in advance, and do this on a weekly basis.
3. Make a list of things you can practice without your instrument.
4. Find an accountability buddy. One of the things that my LMT members find super helpful is having an *accountability buddy*. Reach out in the free Facebook group, or ask someone, for example a family member, to hold you accountable at home.
5. Change your mindset: If you keep telling yourself that you are too busy to practice, it creates a negative habit. It's our habits that keep us from fulfilling our potential.
6. Set yourself a reminder. Mobiles and tablets have the capacity to 'ping' to remind you to do something at a specific time. The good old fashioned method of post-it-notes around the house, works just as well!

The brain carries out your intentions, and as humans, we don't like to be wrong. So, if you keep telling yourself that you're too busy, things are unlikely to change. Try rephrasing it to – 'I would love to do more practice, but 10 minutes is all I can commit to right now.' After all, 10 minutes every day for a month, equals just over four and half hours!

The bottom line is we all have 24 hours in a day; if others can get some practice done and still find time for family and friends, so can you!

Phew! That felt like a real 'dressing down' for my readers, but justified, I think, because one powerful mindset shift, new direction, idea, or tweak in the schedule can change *everything*. The key to making progress with music is to practice little and often. Plan your sessions to have a clear and attainable focus, because success quickly builds motivation and confidence.

Lacking in motivation?
Finding yourself lacking in motivation is also something you are likely to experience at some point on your musical journey. For most of my early years, music practice felt like a frustrating slog, with far too many plateaus and frustrations. Conversations at college with fellow students, frequently centred around the "number of hours" one had done. I remember constantly feeling like I needed to do more, and assumed that was why I wasn't as good as everyone around me.

Looking back, I can see that a lot of this negativity around my practice was not due to the amount of time I was putting in. It was, rather, the lack of significant results I felt I was getting out. Repeating things over and over didn't always work.

Improvements wouldn't stick consistently from one day to the next, and I always lacked confidence. Thankfully, my ways changed when I met Richard Ingham. He made me realise that getting better results from my practice had little to do with the length of practice time. It's about what you do when you practice and the mental approach you take that gets you the desired results.

Once I took this onboard, every practice session made a difference. I improved faster and things stuck from one session to the next. I started to enjoy the process, and my confidence blossomed. It turns out I was more than capable of reaching and surpassing some of the heights that my fellow students around me were attaining.

If you've been feeling down about your practice lately or you are looking for a new approach, here are a few ideas.

1. Lift your mood by playing pieces you already know well. This is an excellent way of boosting your confidence and bringing back some enjoyment into your practice.
2. Find an *accountability partner* to support you. It's been one of the best things that I've introduced as part of my 'Learn Music Together Academy. Sharing your experiences will soon make you realise that you are not alone; practice is not always fun.
3. Take a step back and think about why things aren't going the way you'd like. Do you have the technical capabilities

to play your piece, or would you get more enjoyment from playing something a little easier?

4. Do you see the patterns within the music? If not, spend some time studying the notes away from your instrument.
5. Can you visualise the music? Do your fingers really know their way around the notes.
6. Have you listened to the piece recently for inspiration?
7. Try a completely different style of piece.
8. Practise a duet piece with a fellow learner.

It's easy to get stuck in a mundane practice routine, in which you do the same things day in, day out. If progress is slow, it won't be long before your motivation dwindles. So, how can you *spice things up a bit*? I regularly do a challenge with my Learn Music Together members to show them how to add variety to their practice methods. As a result, the community spirit always reignites, becomes re-energised, everyone supports each other, and the results are sensational.

"It takes several repeats to actually discover what I needed to be listening for. Usually, I can hear the mistakes in the rhythm. But, I needed more deliberate listening to hear the mistake in pitch. this is definitely great practice for me." **Elisa**

"My experience mirrors Elisa's... rhythm is easier, but I was really hitting rewind on pitch. These are great exercises." **Sandy**

"Day 2 complete- absolutely loving this challenge; it's making me so aware of what areas I need to work on further." **Bev**

If you need a few sparks of creativity right now, here are some ideas.

1- **Make a rhythm card.**

These are a fantastic way to practice specific rhythms. First, grab yourself a piece of paper and write out some rhythms that you find challenging. Then, practise clapping the rhythms to a metronome whenever you get the opportunity. Remember to count in the smallest note value, rather than subdivide, as this will help you attain a higher level of precision.

Spot-the-difference tests.

Hearing errors in your playing is super helpful, and as there's so much to think about when we practise, we don't always spot them soon enough. By recording yourself and listening back, you can check to see if you are playing accurately. I created several of what I call **'spot the difference'** exercises for my members to practice. There's one in the extra resources of this book for you try.

Create your own exercises using musical words.

Write yourself a list of words that only use the letters A-G. Here's a few examples: *Bed, Dad, Beef, Fade, Badge, Baggage*

Now it's time to get creative. There are so many things you can practice using these words as a starting point. For example, if you are a beginner, you could spell out the words on your instrument. You could practice playing a particular rhythm on each letter. If you are a bit more advanced, try playing the major chord for each letter or embellishing each letter with an ornament. You could practise different articulation patterns or dynamics.

Here are a few more ideas to get your creative juices flowing.

- Spell out the words on manuscript.
- Repeat step one but using ledger lines.
- Challenge yourself by writing the words out in the alto or tenor clef.
- Spell out the words on your instrument, but play the notes a 3rd - or any interval - higher or lower.
- Play the words in a very high or low register.

- Use harmonics to play the words.
- Play each note in a different octave.
- Play 2 equal notes on each letter, and increase the speed with a metronome.
- Double tongue on each note.
- Triple tongue on each note.
- Play a trill on each note.
- Play a turn on each note.
- Try a mordent on every letter.
- Play a major triad on each letter of the word.
- Play a minor triad on each letter or any other kind of chord you want to practice.
- Practise the major scale for each letter of the word.
- Now practise the minor scale for each letter.
- Practise more challenging scales for each letter, such as arpeggios, wholetone, pentatonic, scales in 3rds, dim 7th's and Dom 7th's.
- Play 4 semiquavers on each letter, alternate fingerings or articulation patterns.
- Play the word in a sequence, ascending then descending.
- Sing the words.
- Compose an 8 or 16 bar melody using the word.
- Play each word staccato or with different bow strokes.
- Play the opening few bars of a well-known tune, starting on each letter of the word.
- Create a lick using the letters of the word.

- Practise your vibrato - play 4 undulations at crotchet = 76, play 3 undulations at crotchet = 100, then do 5 undulations at crotchet = 60.
- Write the major key signature for each letter.
- Write the minor key signature for each letter.

Using these words is an excellent way of improving your skills and raising your awareness. Removing the sheet music allows you to focus on a specific element or technique that you want to improve. They also allow you to get creative which is always a benefit.

Music bingo card.

Another fun way to motivate yourself is to create a *music bingo card*, the idea being to get a full house each week. Use the one below to get started.

Highlighted some music	Created some warm-up exercises	Clapped rhythms with a metronome	Listened to a recording of piece
Made a recording of yourself	Been creative with scales practice daily	Done some sightreading practice	Focused on the dynamics within a piece
Used a metronome every practice session	Practiced the phrasing and articulation	Sang the melody rather than playing it	Made some practise goals for the week
Taken or watched a music lesson	Worked on tone production or balance	Done some theory, composition or improvising	Played along with someone or a backing track

Chapter 18 - Musicality

How do you get that piece to sound musical?

To play musically, you have to know the piece really well. While you don't necessarily have to memorise the notes, you should be able to play them without reading every beat on the page. It's a bit like when you make a speech and have little cards to act as prompt reminders. Here's one of my favourite exercises, that takes random practice one step further. It's a great way of testing how well you really know the music.

- First, take a copy of your music and then cut it into strips (one line at a time).
- Put the strips of music in a bag and shake them up.
- Next time you practise, put your hand in the bag and pull out one of the strips.
- Now, play the 4 bars that precede those on the piece of paper you pulled from the bag. You can also try playing the four bars that follow, which is often easier to do.

If you struggle at first, it's ok to look at your score. If you can't play the bars from memory, see if you can sing them. You'll start to understand and hear the music as part of a larger creative framework. You'll gain a deeper insight into how the parts relate to the unified whole. This is like 'seeing the bigger picture' in aural terms, as an aural landscape, which helps you play more musically. When you know the whole piece and can start from anywhere, you no longer rely on your eyes to read each note individually. Therefore, your brain has more energy for other things, and your creative side will shine through.

Pay attention to the detail in the score.
So often, learners focus solely on playing the right notes with the correct rhythm. However, the articulation and dynamic shades are what transform the piece musically.

To ensure you're getting really clear tonal shades, select bars that have different dynamic markings from your piece and play them one after the other. Let's say bar 1 is forte, bar 5 is piano and bar 9 is mezzo piano. Play each of those bars in turn and focus on making a clear difference in the volume. Then, record those bars and see if you can hear the difference.

Here's another exercise that I love to do with students - you'll need to take a copy of your music and cross out all the dynamic markings for this exercise.

• Next, record your piece using the original music. Make sure you differentiate the changes in dynamic shades when you play.

• Now grab the copy you made of the music, and as you listen back to your recording, see if you can write on the dynamics you hear.

• Finally, compare the two copies of music- did you miss any dynamic shades or get a few wrong?

You can do the same exercise with articulation. Ask yourself if your staccato dots are crisp or how smooth your legato phrases are.

How can you shape a phrase more musically?

Before I continue, let's look at what a musical phrase is?

Phrases in music are the equivalent of sentences in a written language. They differ from a motif in music as they are a complete thought. However, they are not the whole story.

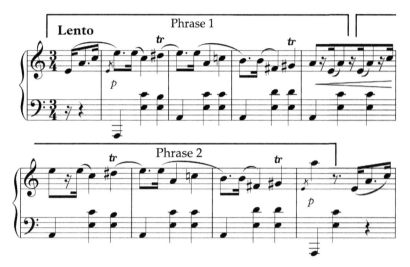

From Chopin Mazurka in A Minor Op.68, No2, bars 1-8

Music uses phrases in a similar way to punctuation in English. We use punctuation to help us understand sentences, while phrases enable us to make sense of melodies. Just imagine if I gave you a piece of text which had no full stops, commas or paragraphs. Then I asked you to read the story on that page to an audience. It would be a tall order. It would be tough to read the story convincingly. You would probably want to grab a pencil before you started, and put in all the necessary punctuation. It's the same in music. It's much harder to play a piece expressively and convince an audience of your message if you can't identify the phrases.

Musical phrases provide shape to sections which, in turn, give structure to the whole work.

Types of Musical Phrases

There are many ways to describe phrases. In general, there are two categories, regular phrasing and irregular phrasing.

Regular Phrasing

Regular phrasing is when the phrase length is the same throughout the piece. In this scenario, phrases are usually two or four bars in length.

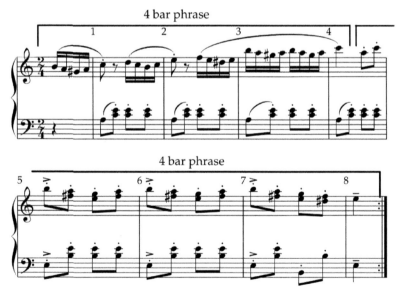

From Mozart, Rondo Alla Turca, Sonata No. 11, K.331, bars 1-8

Recurring Phrasing

Recurring phrasing is also considered as regular phrasing. A recurring phrase is a leitmotif that repeats and is related to a character, place or idea. Leitmotifs are used in opera to unify the work and tell the story without using words.

The operas of Wagner contain some great examples of this type of phrasing. Below, is a leitmotif taken from his opera 'Die Walküre,' the second of four operas that make up the *Ring Cycle*. *The Ride of the Valkyries* comes at the beginning of act two.

Valkyries Ride Theme, From Wagner, Die Walküre WWV 86B

Irregular Phrasing

The opposite of regular phrasing is irregular phrasing, where the phrase lengths vary. The opening of *Chopin's Ballade No. 1, OP. 23 (see image on the next page)* begins with a three-bar phrase followed by a two-bar phrase. You could also argue that this is one complete five-bar phrase. Irregular phrasing in music, was preferred by composers in the romantic period, as these composers, unlike their predecessors, wanted to express themselves with a greater sense of freedom.

From Chopin Ballad Op 23, No1 bars 1 -5

In the classical period, musical structures such as the sonata form were commonplace, but these forms were too restricted for the romantic composers. They favoured more long, expressive melodies with a variety of melodic ideas.

In the romantic era, chromatic passagework and more advanced harmonies gave greater tonal colour, to the emotion or narrative content of the music. This new level of musical expression, extended beyond the scope and confines of the more traditional, classical forms, and needed phrasing with fewer cadential points.

How to identify phrases in music?

Identifying the musical phrases of a song is a great place to start, when learning to recognise them. The text effortlessly defines the phrases related to music. For example:

Three blind mice,

Three blind mice,

See how they run,

at the end of each line, there is a natural place to take a breath. However, we know that this is not the end of the rhyme, as there is no full stop. Similarly, the first line (three blind mice) would represent a phrase, not the end of the piece.

Identifying phrases for music in various time signatures.

Most musicians would agree that you can identify the end of a phrase by a cadence. Musical cadences represent the commas and full stops. A cadence is a progression of two chords, which either makes the piece or section feel finished or unfinished.

From Beethoven Bagatelle Op.119, No.1, bars 1-8

250

It is common in music for the start of each phrase to begin in the same or similar way. The piece below has two four-bar phrases which are easy to identify as each one begins with an anacrusis (an upbeat).

From Fauré, Sicilienne Op. 78, bars 1-9 in treble clef

In the previous two examples, the anacrusis makes it easy for us to identify the phrases. For music that starts on the beat, though, how do we know where the phrase begins and ends? The Minuet below, by Mozart has two four-bar phrases.

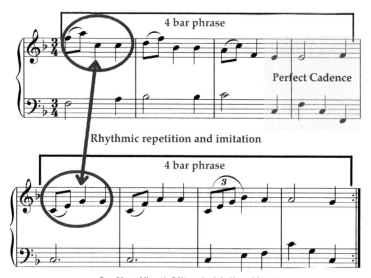

From Mozart Minuet in F, K2, notebook for Nannerl, bars 1-8

251

Two things help us define the phrases of this piece. The first is the clear cadence at the end of bar four. The second is the use of rhythmic repetition or imitation. The start of the second phrase, while not the same as the first, is similar. In classical music, this is often the case, although not always so.

Antecedent and Consequent Music Phrases
These terms describe question and answer phrases. Composers use them in all genres, mainly when there is a prominent melody. Hence you'll find examples in pop, jazz, rock and classical music, to name but a few. Antecedent and consequent phrases often - but not always begin - in the same way. When we hear them, they sound similar but we instantly recognise that they are different. Why?

The antecedent phrase leaves the listener feeling abandoned because the music feels unfinished. If a performer were to play only the antecedent phrase and then walk off stage, the audience would feel unsatisfied. Below is the antecedent phrase at the start of *Mozart's Symphony No 40*.

Opening theme from Mozart Symphony No 40, K550 bars 1-5

There is an expectation that the music will continue. The underlying harmony is responsible for this as an antecedent phrase in music doesn't end on the tonic. Instead, there is an imperfect cadence or half close, as some people refer to it.

The consequent phrase brings the conclusion, there's a perfect or authentic cadence at the end which satisfies the listener. Here is the consequent phrase to Mozart's opening of his *Symphony No 40.*

Opening theme from Mozart Symphony No 40, K550 bars 5-9

The consequent phrase complements the antecedent phrase: when you hear them together, you know they belong as one.
If the answer to the antecedent phrase begins with the same rhythm and pitch, the response is called a parallel consequent. An example of this would be the 'Ode to Joy theme' in *Beethoven's Symphony No 9.*

From Beethoven Symphony No. 9, Op. 125 fourth movement

You could describe the antecedent and consequent phrases as one long phrase. They are often used as a repeated phrase in music to form a theme within a section.

Tip!

Look for bars of music which are very similar, but perhaps the final bar is different.

What are balanced phrases in music?

The antecedent and consequent phrases are an example of balanced phrases. The consequent phrase balances and is almost symmetrical to the antecedent phrase apart from the cadence point. The two phrases together make what's called a 'period' in music. The period is often doubled to form a musical section.

Extended Phrases

Extended phrases often reiterate a motive (motif) of a phrase before the cadence, or where you would expect the cadence to fall. The phrase is therefore extended, meaning the cadence is delayed.

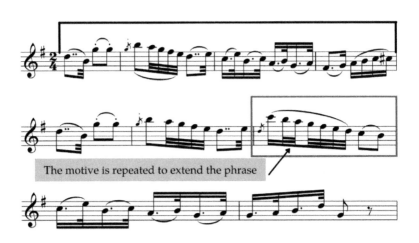

From Haydn's Symphony No.101 in D Major, Hob 1:101, second movement, bars 2-9

Another way composers extend the phrase is by repeating the final cadence or prolonging the sense of closure towards the end of a phrase, section or piece.

Musical Phrasing Techniques

When you can identify phrases, the next step is to shape them while playing. All phrases have a centre, or a climactic point, that the musical energy directs itself towards or disperses from. The notes within a phrase are either: leading to the climax, at the climatic point or descending from the climax.

The energy that disperses from this climactic point defines the shape of the phrase.

How do I shape a phrase in music?
There are many ways that you can shape a phrase in music, and often there are several options which all work musically. It comes down to personal choice, and the musical intentions you want to convey.

Dynamics
The easiest way to add colour to the melodic line is to use dynamics. The most common way is to crescendo towards the centre of a phrase, and then diminuendo afterwards.

Tapering the ends of phrases with musical control, is something that takes years of practice and lots of listening. The best way to improve, if you are playing a wind, brass or string instrument, is by practising long notes which crescendo or diminuendo. Aim to keep the tone quality the same, no matter what dynamic you are playing. The skill is to make the change in dynamics as gradual as possible. Try and crescendo to your loudest or diminuendo to you softest point, without losing the tone quality of the note. Often, learners go louder or softer too abruptly, so the subtle tonal colours are lost.

On the piano or guitar, you need to practise the hand and arm movements at the start and end of the phrase. Small gestures and movements can help ensure that the phrase contours are controlled and exquisitely managed. You can also highlight the centre of a phrase by a sudden change in dynamic. In this instance, it can be effective to use a diminuendo as you approach the centre of the phrase, and then use an unexpected accent to highlight the energetic point. The damper pedal on the piano can also be used to enhance a crescendo or diminuendo.

Rubato

Rubato is another way that musicians shape phrases to describe musical emotion. The tempo becomes slightly quicker towards the centre of the phrase and slows back down after the central point. Each phrase may have a different feel ebb and flow depending upon the energy the player is trying to create.

Tip!

Before adding rubato, make sure you can play the piece in time with a metronome. What often happens when learners deploy rubato without being able to fully control the rhythm, is they slow down at the more challenging bars, as opposed to where the energy slows in the music. You should employ the same method when practising a bar that is marked rall. (rallentando) or rit. (ritardando). First practise the bar at the correct tempo, then see if you can gradually slow down the notes.

Vibrato

Using vibrato is a fantastic way of adding shape and definition to a phrase. You might widen the vibrato or increase the speed as the energy intensifies. Again care needs to be taken to ensure that you can control the vibrato. If it becomes too wide, the intonation is often compromised. On the other hand, if it is too tight, the tone can sound restricted.

How do you choose what to do?

There is no easy answer to this as one of the great things about music is that it's open to interpretation. A professional musician will make something feel natural and shape phrases in a way that is unique to them. The more you listen to music, the deeper your musical understanding of phrase shaping and tonal colour will become. If you are at the start of your musical journey, keep things simple. Try doing a crescendo to the midpoint of the phrase, and diminuendo towards the end.

If you're a little more advanced, you could add some vibrato or rubato if the music lends itself to those techniques.

Don't be afraid to experiment with phrasing. If you don't like something, you can always change it again. No two musical performances are the same, but the best ones are those in which the performer commits and believes in what they are doing. Musicians who can draw their listeners in and connect with their hearts are the true masters. Don't be too hard on yourself if you feel you've still got a long way to go - communicating your musical intentions takes years of practice.

Dynamic shades throughout your music as a whole.

When it comes to redecorating, choosing colours is something I ponder over for hours. Even if you are a magnolia type of person, there are so many subtle shades with names that either entice or repel you. When choosing colours, you try to visualise your room and talk to yourself – 'that's too cold, too bright, too yellow, too pink' and finally, you choose something you hope will be the perfect fit.

Colour in music also makes a massive difference to the overall musicality of your playing. Learners often ask me how to play more musically, and as with paint, dynamic shades make a difference.

Ask yourself questions such as:

'Where are the emotional intensities within the music, and how can I vary the volume?' Such questions are great starting points. If you are not sure, here are a few guidelines to help.

Listen to the whole piece.

When actors receive a script, they don't immediately start to learn their lines. They begin by getting an overview of the story and research the characters. Without this knowledge, they would be unable to learn their lines with the right emotions. You need to make similar connections when learning music. When you analyse your music, think about how you will capture the mood, style, tempo and tonal colours. You can do this by listening to recordings, studying the score and researching the context of the music.

Graduate the dynamics to convey the emotion of the piece as a whole.
As a general rule, more volume intensifies the emotional power of the music. Melodies that ascend often grow in intensity, while descending phrases often offer repose. The harmony also drives the intensity of the music. As the music travels away from the tonic and primary chords (I, IV and V), the power increases significantly. So again, you can adjust your volume accordingly, getting louder as you move away from the tonic and softer as the music returns.

Find the climactic part of the music.
It depends upon the style of music that you are playing, and not every piece will have a climactic point. If it does, these notes should be the loudest. Mark this section on the music, and graduate the rest of your dynamics accordingly.

Have fun and get creative. Don't be afraid to experiment and let go. So often, there is a tendency with learners to do 'only' what it says on the music - and no more. The score markings are a guideline, just as a tin of tomatoes is the base of a bolognese sauce. However, to elevate that bolognese sauce into something memorable, you have to add additional ingredients. It's the same with music.

> **To create shape and intensity, you have to add a variety of dynamic shades.**

Unleashing Your Musicality

A fantastic exercise that allows you to tap into your creative side is to play a piece that you know well, and instead of worrying about all the right notes in the right place, try this:

Change the Piece's Character: Play the piece in a way that it wasn't intended to be played. Make it an angry piece, a march, play it in a jazz style, or with a romantic feel. At first you may find this challenging. You have to let go of your inhibitions, and have some fun. For many it will mean stepping outside of your comfort zone, but believe me it works. Get creative; imagine you are a ballerina gracefully moving across the floor, or a clown entertaining your audience at the circus. After going through the exercise several times with different characters, play your piece in the style that the composer intended. You'll often find that it sounds much more musical.

Elevating a Piece Further.

Lots of people find themselves in a dilemma about how much to challenge themselves musically. It's a fine line. If you choose a piece that's too hard, then progress is slow. However, **when you can play a piece, how do you elevate it even further?**
Many of you have pieces that you can play, yet you still want to improve them. When you can play a piece reasonably well, you are unlikely to focus as much when you practise. Unfortunately, that means that it's easier for errors to creep their way back in, or you may overlook the performance detail in the music. To heighten your focus and challenge yourself further, here are a few ideas to try.

Change the Articulation: If your piece is *legato,* try playing it *staccato.* If you play an instrument such as the piano, take this one step further by keeping one hand legato and making the other hand play staccato. You can also try mixing the articulation patterns, for example - two notes slurred and two notes detached etc. You'll find that you have to really focus, but you'll discover which bars you know well and which bars, perhaps, need more work.

Change the Dynamics: Play the piece, but use the opposite dynamics to what the music says. So, if the music begins forte, start piano. It's great fun and can often result in a much wider array of tonal shades.

Change the Tempo – Halve the metronome speed or double it, and see if you can still play in time. If you know the notes well, you should be able to play them at any speed, so this is another excellent way to discover which bars still need further practice.

Play with a Distraction - Put the radio or television on really loud, and try playing your piece. Or get someone to talk to you or make an annoying noise. These types of distractions will challenge your level of focus at first, but with practice you can learn to ignore them and focus solely on your music. If you have a performance coming up, this exercise is highly recommended.

The takeaway here is to *Get creative*; you could double all the time values or play the piece in a swing style. Challenging yourself to think differently makes you concentrate on a deeper level, plus it unleashes your musicality. When you've finished your practice, play the piece as it should be and see if the notes flow with more ease.

Elevating music to another level and adding personal touches is the reason professional musicians sound so good. It's not a gift or a special talent. It's years of creative thinking and practice, which means you can do it too.

Chapter 19 - Memorisation

Memorising music gives you the ultimate level of freedom and expression when you perform. While I don't think it is necessary to perform from memory in a concert, I believe that you should regularly invest the time to memorise pieces during your practice. For many people, the process of memorising anything can be overwhelming and daunting. However, we are all capable of developing our memory, and with the correct methods, it is something that you can achieve.

When it comes to memorising, it's essential to understand that there are many methods that you can try. What works for one person doesn't necessarily work for another. So if you have tried before, without success, know that it isn't because you *can't* memorise, it's because you used the wrong method for *you*.

It's also essential to remember that you can't go from zero to a hundred overnight if you are new to memorisation. Like anything else, it takes regular practice to develop the skills.

There are four stages to memorising a piece of music, so if you have solely relied on repetition in the past, this may come as a pleasant surprise.

Research suggests that we forget approximately 50% of what we learn within an hour and, on average, 70% within 24 hours. To memorise anything, you have to recall it *regularly*.

Memory Exercises

Training your memory is something you can do, whether it be memorising music or item on a shopping list. If you want to try some fun exercises to help develop your memory skills, check out humanbenchmark.com.

Stage 1 -Awareness and Perception

Understanding the structure of a composition is something professionals can do at a glance. However, as a learner this awareness is something you have to learn how to develop.

To memorise a piece, you have to spend time mapping out the structure. When I use coloured boxes to mark music, I am bringing things to my attention in a very visual way. (Refer to chapter to 3 for an example).

You need to have a clear understanding of the musical components.

Below are a few examples of things you could map out.
• Bars or sections that repeat
• Scale patterns or motifs that occur within the music
• Harmonic progressions, rhythmic repetition, sequences, imitations, and the phrase structure.
• The key and modulations the piece travels through.
• The mood you are trying to convey in each section.
• Where does the climax occur within each phrase?
• What articulation patterns does the music have and do they change.
• How the motif or theme appears within the textural balance.

Create a mind map

Mind maps are a visual way of mapping out the music. You can use symbols, shapes and colours to draw a 'map' of the key features of your piece. If you are practising a large scale work, start by creating a mind map of each section. Then, create an additional mind map for the work as a whole.

On the next page you'll find the sheet music for *a Hungarian Folksong by Bartók* and an example of a mind map for this piece opposite it. There is no right or wrong way to use the shapes and symbols, so use whatever works best for you.

From Bartók, Hungarian Folksong, The first term at the piano, Sz.53

Mind map of Bartók Hungarian Folksong.

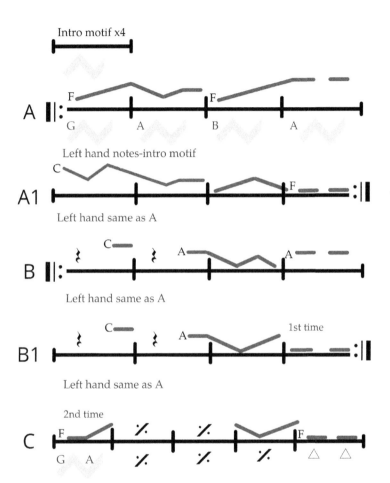

268

As well as a structural map, you also need to have a technical map.

The best way to do this is by visualising yourself playing the piece.

Ask yourself questions like:

• Am I confident with the fingering patterns?

• Do I know where to take a breath, use the pedal, or what bow stroke I am using?

• Am I confident with the tempo changes, tricky rhythms or coordination challenges?

• Where am I going to change the tonal colours, and how am I going to do that?

Stage 2 - Encoding the Music

Someone adept at memorising doesn't just repeat things until they think they know it. They use aural and conceptual memory to internalise the framework of the *entire composition*.

One of the reasons people crumble under pressure in lessons is because they've learnt a piece by solely repeating it, mindlessly in practice. They haven't got any of the *mental hooks* in place to latch onto under pressure. Things such as fingering patterns, notes and rhythms were learnt unconsciously through blocked practice methods. Hence, under pressure they can't retrieve them.

The key ingredient here is to create meaning within the music. To memorise something, it has to be more than a series of notes that you've learnt through repetitive practice.

Start with a plan.

Memorise a short section of music each practice. I would suggest you start with the 4 bars or a phrase that you have been practising.

To do this:

1. Visualise the music shortly after you've practised it and then again later in the day.
2. Recall it once more the following day.
3. If any part is vague or you are unsure, revisit the score and look over the notes. Then try and visualise it again.

Don't try and memorise too much. The brain can only take *on board* a certain amount of information in one sitting. If you try and do too much, you'll exceed your threshold, and everything you've learnt will become muddled. It's like building a stack of cards. When you put one too many on the tower collapses. For more information on creating meaning to what you are trying to learn, I highly recommend Jim Kwik's book *'Limitless'*. It's not specifically about music, but he does give some great exercises that you can use, whatever you are trying to learn.

Visualise and Play

Take a few bars of music and visualise the notes. If anything isn't clear, refer to the score. As you visualise, make sure you vocalise the note names, count out the rhythms and recall the articulation patterns. Mental practice is one of the key ingredients to memorising music, but it must be done regularly. It's something that you should start doing in the early stages of learning a piece, and you should try to maintain daily. Try miming the playing with your fingers, and then see if you can sing the melody in tune. Once you're confident that you can visualise the music, try to play the bars, accurately and at a steady tempo, several times on your instrument.

Over the next few practises, link segments together, overlapping them to ensure fluency. Then, join the parts into larger sections. If there are weak areas, revisit the visualisation method for those few bars, and consult the score if necessary. Repeat each memorised section several times regularly. Ensure that you keep the tempo steady and play accurately. Aim to convey more expression and play with greater ease on each attempt.

Involve other methods too
Aural Awareness
Practice hearing the music in your head. Think ahead to the next phrase, and test yourself by starting at different sections in the music.

Overall Framework
Think about where each section/phrase appears in the overall structure. At first, you can do this by copying the music and cutting it up into phrases. Put the bits of paper in a bag and pull out a phrase at random. Then play the phrase that comes before or after that in the piece.

Handwrite the music
One of the most effective ways to consolidate memory recall is to write out the music on manuscript paper. See if you can do this every day with your 4 bars of music that you are trying to memorise.

Don't just think about the melody.
Vocalise the accompaniment as well as the melody. This applies to instruments as well. Make sure you know the parts of any accompanying instruments, and also what happens in the music during any bars of rest.

Stage 3 - Preservation
Once you've memorised the music, you need to exercise the brain cells regularly to stay alert. If you don't, they'll be redirected elsewhere to perform other tasks. You should also be aware that casually running through a piece from memory won't preserve the material either. It's essential to engage the cognitive side of the brain, so don't become reliant on the motor skills. You need to be constantly aware of the intricate detail within the music. These include the technical, structural and stylistic information you mapped out in the awareness and perception stage.

Muscle memory alone is not enough.
If you place one finger in the wrong place, you will likely crumble if your conscious memory is not alert.
Your memory will be more efficient when new musical and technical discoveries heighten it.

- Try playing sections of the piece at different tempos.
- Mime yourself playing in an understated way or exaggerate the movements.
- Change the dynamics and articulation.
- Practise performing to someone, then ask yourself questions such as the ones below.
- Were you able to visualise ahead?
- Were there any sketchy passages or memory lapses? If so, revisit the perception and ingraining techniques.
- Isolate sections of the music and practise with only one hand, or play the rhythm on one note. Ask yourself if you can – Play with the left hand, while singing the right-hand melody. Can you hear the accompaniment as you play?
- Record yourself playing and listen back.
- Revisit the score and look for new possibilities and ideas in the music.

Stage 4 - Recall

Recalling music confidently is, of course, what you are striving for when you memorise a piece. You can be confident that you have reached this stage when you can play the notes with ease, think on a multidimensional level, and you are in complete control of your playing.

Playing with Ease

- In the practice room, can you start from any beat within any bar?
- Can you imagine the music in your mind with little effort?

Multidimensional

The musical structure, techniques and expression are all incorporated. For example:

• You can play hands separately.

• You can play with or without the pedal.

• You can vocalise the letter names of the notes in any part of the piece.

• You know how the phrases relate to each other.

• You can pull a phrase out of your bag and know exactly where that fits in the music.

• You can talk your way through the piece and describe it in detail to somebody else.

Complete Control

• You can do more than just what it says on the page.

• You can play the piece at different speeds.

• You can change the dynamics and articulation patterns if you choose.

• You can play any semiquaver passagework with a variety of rhythms.

• You can play the piece super slowly with a metronome (I'm talking crotchet = 40) without any errors.

Finally, you have to continually work on your mindset to recall things that you've memorised successfully. Don't let negative thoughts take over, and always maintain fluency if you have memory hiccups. Keep working on performance anxieties and include exercises to control your nerves.

If you develop the practice methods outlined in this book, you will be developing all the necessary skills required to memorise music.

Section 5

Perform and Grow

Chapter 20 - Performing

Before you close this book or skip this chapter, people often tell me that they have no desire to perform. However, I disagree with that thought. In my experience, lack of confidence and self-belief, rather than lack of desire, is often what leads you to think this way. When you conquer the former, the latter has room to flourish. Like many things, it's the fear of failure that convinces the mind that performance is beyond our capabilities. When you initially began your musical journey, somewhere in your dream you hoped that, one day, you would reach a standard where people would enjoy listening to you. That doesn't necessarily mean that you want to be a concert pianist performing on a big stage, but we all have that pipe dream – often not consciously acknowledged – of entertaining friends and family.

Performing is one of the best ways to make progress. Nothing grows your confidence like the smiles and compliments you receive from your listeners.

Music is a gift and one which is meant to be shared. Like all gifts, there is more pleasure in the giving than there is in the receiving. So often, it's people's fears, past experiences, egos and anxieties that prevent us from sharing music.

As we get older, our confidence diminishes, especially in fields where we lack experience. We don't want to feel foolish, so we tell ourselves that we are not good enough to perform.

Conquering those fears is one of the areas I focus on in my 'Learn Music Together' Academy. Every month, I write an arrangement for my members, and they record their parts. My partner and I then compile a professional video for members to share with others. Not only do members find that their rhythmic skills and confidence improve, they see how much joy the music brings to those they share it with. Furthermore, they soon learn that they are now inspiring other adult learners, which is the most powerful gift that music offers. Alison came along to one of my masterclasses; here's her account of the experience -

"I got overwhelmed tonight when watching and hearing the ensemble perform 'Amazing Grace' and the realisation that I was able to do that. As you rightly remembered, I haven't performed publicly since the Brownies (approx. 47 years ago), and my confidence in playing in front of friends or family has diminished, in line with my general ability over the years. I'd reached a stage of not performing to anyone except my husband and preferring him to be in another room doing something else. I've really picked it up properly over the last 18 months, and not only am I more comfortable playing with my husband around, I've fought my inhibitions, and have recently played to my elderly parents which gave them joy (after all they sacrificed a lot to afford for their 4 daughters to all have lessons for 12 years or so). I listened to your FB video a week or so ago and again this morning, about overcoming performance anxiety, and you'd said that you think, deep down, we've all got that desire to be able to perform. The pressure to play for others had become a very big thing that was playing (excuse the pun) on my mind, massively, and *was holding me back from practising and playing at all. So, for the last few years, I've told myself I absolutely don't need/have to perform for anyone I just want to play for my own pleasure. This is still true: there is no requirement to perform at all. My requirement is purely for my own satisfaction, but hearing the ensemble tonight and your FB video this morning, has made me realise it will add to my satisfaction to play with others and to be able to perform. It's also the realisation that 'performing' doesn't have to be at concert pianist standard, a point you made exceptionally well in your FB video; that's a misconception I'd got stuck in my mind. You unlocked a lot of emotions for me tonight which I truly hadn't expected. I'm definitely on a journey, and it's a very exciting one."* **Alison K**

That is one of the most heartfelt emails I've ever received, and by sharing it here, Alison, you are inspiring others.

Performing is a word that has so many connotations attached to it. For most adults, past experiences of feeling anxious, sounding terrible, or feeling like they let themselves down come flooding back. The barriers immediately go up, and while you might not think they are compromising your progress, they truly are. If you believe you are not good enough to perform, then you will never unlock your true potential.

You are also missing out on a whole new level of enjoyment. LMT members regularly play to one another online, and several get great pleasure in performing to those who most benefit. Elderly people in care homes, people in hospices, church communities, local communities, all love listening to music that they are familiar with. Forget about performing Beethoven's most complex works; think about how much people love to just sing along to well-known tunes.

Sharing music is all about the listener, not about yourself. The problem with performance is that people's egos get in the way. They feel the need to push themselves way beyond their technical capabilities, which is why they fail to enjoy the performance. To truly immerse yourself in the music, you need to perform pieces that you can play with ease.

On the flip side of the coin, people really don't make a point of listening for mistakes when they hear music. Think about it for a moment; why do you listen to music? It's often to support the emotion that you are currently feeling. You probably have a playlist for all moods - songs that cheer you up when you're feeling down, songs that seem to be in sympathy with your own sadness, or tunes that fill you with joy when you're feeling happy. I bet you don't have a playlist for listening to spot errors and faults with other performers.

Getting Started with Sharing Music

One of the best ways to make progress on an instrument is by playing alongside others. Not only do you instantly feel more confident having someone to play alongside, you also learn a lot more. An ensemble acts like a warm, cosy blanket which you can wrap around yourself. It provides comfort and support.

Here are a few more benefits of playing in an ensemble:

- **Develops Self-Confidence** - When you perform with others, you realise that you are contributing to something that is much greater as a whole.

- **Improves your Listening Skills** - There are lots of parts within a band; you are like a piece of a jigsaw puzzle. You learn how to listen to other instruments and align your part with theirs.

- **Communication** - You'll learn from the conductor how to interpret their instructions. You'll also gain a greater understanding of rhythm and the importance of the downbeat.

- **Learn from Others** - Following the lead from those who are better than you, is a great way to improve. By listening to the way others play, you'll develop all aspects of your technique.

- **Meet Like-Minded People** - An ensemble is a great social opportunity to make new friends; people like you who understand the challenges of learning to play an instrument. You'll have the opportunity to share your stories and enjoy playing music together. There's a real sense of pride when you are part of a community; you enjoy a sense of belonging; it's an environment in which you can be nurtured, grow and thrive.

- **Broaden your Musical Palette** - We often play the same style of music when learning alone. Within an ensemble, you'll broaden your musical vocabulary. There may be the opportunity to learn new techniques and discover new music.

- **Musical Awareness** - As you gain a deeper understanding of how the roles of different instruments work within an ensemble, you'll learn more about textural balance and how this is created. This will spill over into your solo playing and have a positive effect.
- **More Joy** - Playing in an ensemble is fun. Sure, it can be hard work, but you'll experience better progress, not only individually, but as a group. You'll also enjoy the experience of performing in concerts and sharing your music with others.

If you play the piano, it can be more challenging to find a group to play with. Ask around and see if you can find a duet partner or join the 'Learn Music Together' Academy. I have lots of pianists who participate each month in our ensembles.

Overcoming Performance Nerves.
Whenever you play for others, you will feel nervous. It's a good thing: it shows that you care about your performance. Confidence comes from the knowledge that you can succeed, so here are a few tips to begin with -

Accept that you will make mistakes
I've put this one top of the list, as I know many people suffer from nerves when they go to a lesson, never mind when they are performing to others. Even professionals make mistakes; the big difference is they don't let them affect the rest of the performance. They let go immediately and stay focused. As soon as you dwell on an error, you are no longer concentrating

on what lies ahead. Consequently, further mistakes happen, and there's the possibility that you will start to panic. It can be a vicious cycle that quickly spirals.

Choose pieces that you can play with ease.
Always perform pieces that are below your technical ability. If you choose music that is at the cusp of your technique, you will be on edge right from the start. You'll be so focused on not making an error that there'll be no space to enjoy the music.

Practice Performing
There are different skills required to perform a piece, and just because you can play it in the practice room, that doesn't mean you can play it under pressure. When we are nervous, our bodies react in a different way. You might have to deal with sweaty palms or an accelerated heartbeat. Some people feel nauseous, while others feel giddy. These are all things that we don't experience in the practice room, and if we don't prepare, they can take over.

Memorise the Piece
I'm not suggesting here that you perform from memory, but you need to know the music well enough to mean that your eyes don't need to be fixated on the page. Far too often, people rely on muscle memory, thinking that this is enough to play with accuracy under pressure. Unfortunately, it's the worst thing to rely on. You should be able to vividly describe your music before you perform under pressure. Mental practice and

some of the exercises I shared in chapter 13, are great ways to memorise the notes.

Meditation Exercises

Many professional musicians and sportspeople practice mediation to control their thoughts. Whether you prefer yoga, Tai Chi or something similar, learning to control your breathing through exercises will help you relax and turn negative thoughts into positive ones.

Visualisation

Visualising your performance beforehand is another powerful way to overcome anxiety. Imagine yourself playing in the environment you are about to perform in. See the audience before you, and imagine them smile as you entertain them with your wonderful music. See yourself playing through the notes and enjoying yourself. Visualise how successful your performance will be and imagine what people will say to you afterwards.

Practice being out of your comfort zone regularly, as this helps you cope under pressure.

Get comfortable with being uncomfortable.

One of the reasons I love to travel off the beaten track is that it has taught me resilience (something I didn't think I had!). As humans, we have an instinct to survive, so believe in yourself. The upside of performing is the incredible rush of adrenaline that you get from the experience. For musicians, it's addictive, and, while the nerves never disappear, the more you perform, the easier it gets. While you might be learning for fun or as a hobby, friends and family will inevitably want to hear you play. So bite the bullet, and prepare a performance for them - if you haven't done so already.

Exercises to improve your focus and conquer those anxieties

1. Your heart rate is likely to increase when you are nervous, so recreating this feeling at home will help you prepare. Do some exercise before you practise. You need to increase your heart rate until you are out of breath. For some, that may mean climbing the stairs a couple of times; for others, you may need to go for a run. Whichever way you exercise, you want to significantly increase your heart rate. Then without cooling down, pick up your instrument, and play through your piece. When you first try this, you'll probably make a number of mistakes. These can often be in places where errors have never happened before. With practice, you can learn to maintain focus while slowing down your heart rate with deeper breaths.

2. Put the radio or television on, at quite a loud volume, and see if you can play through your piece. At first, you may find that you get distracted listening to the background noise. It may be that the tune on the radio is at a completely different tempo to your piece, and you'll find it hard to maintain a consistent pulse.

3. I've mentioned this exercise earlier, but I'll reiterate it here as it's great for improving your focus and awareness.

Perform your piece while standing on one leg. Or get a friend to try and distract you while you are playing. It's not uncommon for people to take photographs when performing in public. The flash of a camera can easily disrupt your concentration, so get a friend to get *snap-happy* as you perform in your practice sessions.

4. Give yourself a reward. When I do this with kids, I use money as a reward, but for adults, you need to find something that's an appropriate treat for yourself.. Chocolates are usually a good idea. You are going to perform your piece 3 times in quick succession. If you play the piece accurately on your first attempt, you get a reward - in my example, one chocolate. On your second attempt, you will get another chocolate if you play accurately, but if you make an error, you will have to forfeit your first chocolate. This creates some pressure and anxiety, so you'll have to raise your level of focus to achieve the reward. If you succeed and make no mistakes, you'll now have two chocolates. Hence the pressure increases on your third attempt as you could lose everything. Remember to be honest with yourself; any slip or flaw is counted as an error. You are aiming to deliver your best performance under pressure, so it's important that the reward is something you desire. Hence, this is why money works so well with children.

On the day of a performance.

Resist the temptation to do lots of rehearsal - if you don't know it by now, then it is too late. If you must run through your piece, do so slowly. Avoid drinking any alcohol. It is totally false that it calms your nerves. It will make your reaction times slower, and you'll be less focused. Do some breathing exercises regularly throughout the day, and imagine yourself delivering your performance ... take a deep breath here ... calmly! BREATHE! Always eat properly on the day of a performance, and avoid foods that will give you quick energy boosts. They may be great initially, but your blood sugar will drop quicker. Slow releasing energy foods such as porridge are much better. Finally make sure you get a good night's sleep; the body needs rest if it's to perform at its best.

At the end of your performance, don't rush off; enjoy chatting to your audience. See what they have to say about your performance. You could be taken by surprise; even if you think you didn't play to your best, it doesn't mean that others will know. So often, we can be overly critical. A listener has no preconceptions; they are unlikely to know if you made a mistake, particularly if you master the art of playing mistakes *well.*

Whenever you perform, you are more likely to remember what went wrong before you celebrate all the bits that went well. Try and conquer this habit. For every negative thought that you recall at the end of your performance, think of a positive moment to celebrate. A day or two later, write an evaluation of your performance. Think about what aspects went well, and what you could improve next time. Write down how you felt before, during and after the performance. Did you suffer from any performance nerves? How did those nerves present themselves? We all think that we'll remember these things, but we rarely do, so keeping performance evaluations is a valuable asset in your preparation going forward.

Fulfil Your Musical Potential!

With the 'Learn Music Together' Academy, you can nurture and grow your practice skills. Like Dolores, Sandy, Alison and the many other students that I mention in this book, YOU TOO can perform with confidence and bring joy to others through your music.

You may have to change your mindset, you'll probably have to step outside your comfort zone and you're bound to experience hurdles along the way, but those who find the patience, resilience and dedication to ride the underlying waves of their musical journey, will discover the magical places that only music can reach.

Choose unlimited possibilities.

Chapter 21 - Choose Unlimited Possibilities

It's time to find a new musical you!

I've poured my heart and soul into the pages of this book because I truly believe that everyone has musical potential.

I wanted to share the best ways to practice with all and anyone who would listen.

I want music to make a difference in your life, and more importantly-

I want you to be able to share your musical skills to make a difference in someone else's life.

Nothing touches the heart as powerfully as a musical performance.

I want you to let the music flow with ease, fluency, precision, and confidence from your fingertips. I want to make it easier for you to fulfil your musical potential. As you know, it's not as easy as it sounds. Practising is not always fun, but it's so worth it when you hear the applause of others at the end of a performance.

I know you can do it!

All you have to do is follow the LMT roadmap that I have presented to you in this book.

With every new piece you learn, aim to strengthen and develop your practice methods. The key is to *take action*. Don't be afraid of going back and consolidating your technique with easier music. Don't be afraid of changing the way you practice.

Make the commitment to yourself. Decide today that you will share the gift of music with others.

You picked up this book for a reason. It sparked your interest because you have a dream to raise your hand with confidence and say, '*I can play*.' Whether it's for the local church service, a community fundraising event, entertaining friends or simply for yourself, make your playing bring enjoyment and touch the heart of others.

The door is open.

The decision to enter is yours.

The Learn Music Together Academy

The Learn Music Together Academy was formed by myself with the specific aim of helping adults to practice better and gain musical confidence.

If you are interested in joining, you can learn more by visiting: https://learnmusictogether.com/membership
Regardless of whether or not you want

to join us at the Learn Music Together Academy, I want to hear your success stories!

I would like to thank you for reading my book!

Your feedback means a lot to me, and I would love to hear what you have to say about the ideas, advice, tips and tricks etc.

I hope you will send me a note, telling me how your practice is going and how your playing has changed as a result of implementing practice methods that work.

You can reach me at fiona@learnmusictogether.com

Here's to you becoming a confident player! And here's to you being able to Play Music Better.

Get Access to training videos, resources and Free Audiobook!

Just to say thank you for buying my book, I would like to give you some extra video resources and my audiobook 100% FREE! The text is fully searchable in the audiobook, so you can quickly find those paragraphs that you want to read again.

TO DOWNLOAD GO TO:
https://playmusicbetterbook.com/ resources or use the QR code.

Notes on Sources

CHAPTER 1

For more on the truth that everybody has the potential to be good at music and *"skill is myelin insulation that wraps neural circuits, and that grows according to certain signals."* See David Coyle, *The Talent Code* (UK, Penguin Random House, 2009), 33.

To learn more about the ten thousand hours of practice, see Malcolm Gladwell *Outliers: The Story of Success* (New York: Little, Brown, 2008).

CHAPTER 4

The studies show that spaced learning improves your retention. For more see Buch, Claudino, Quentin, Bönstrup, Cohen, *Consolidation of human skill linked to waking hippocampo - neocortical replay*, cell reports, volume 35, issue 10, 109193, available at cell.com.

Michael Boettcher, Johannes Boettcher, Stefan Mietzsch, Thomas Krebs, Robert Bergholz, Konrad Reinshagen, *The spaced learning concept significantly improves training for laparoscopic suturing: a pilot randomized controlled study*, Surgical endoscopy volume 32, pgs. 154-159 and the research article *Synaptic evidence for the efficacy of spaced learning* available online at pnas.org.

For a comprehensive understanding of the importance of sleep, I highly recommend the book by Matthew Walker, *Why we Sleep: The New Science of Sleep and Dreams* (Penguin books 2018) e-book edition 111-112

If you add a little to a little and do this often, soon the little will become great by Hesiod available from https://quotefancy.com/quote/ 1707390/, October 2021

Many musicians are fixated on complex elements that they fail to spend enough time on the basics and if you don't stay with the material long

enough for it to become comfortable, you'll find that it doesn't stay with you
extract from Kenny Werners' excellent book, *Effortless Mastery* (Jamey Aebersold Jazz, 1996) pg. 60.

Duke Ellington Quote - https://www.brainyquote.com/quotes/duke_ellington_167448 (October 28th 2021)

CHAPTER 5

To maximise your time, succeed and live your best life, visit michaelhyatt.com and read his book, *Your Best Year Ever, A 5 step plan for achieving your most important goals* (Baker books 2018).

My email's final quotation that Clive refers to: *So often, people's fears, past experiences, egos, and anxieties prevent them from sharing music. As we get older, our confidence diminishes, especially in fields where we lack experience. Page 64.* If you would like to receive weekly practice tips visit https://playmusicbetter.com/resources

To learn more about committing to your goals see the research by Dr. Gail Matthews, a psychology professor at the Dominican University in California.

Ben D Gardner study at the University College of London, Busting the 21 days habit formation myth (29th June 2012) available online UCL blog https://blogs.ucl.ac.uk/bsh/tag/66-days/.

CHAPTER 6

For more information and links to several research and university articles evidencing why you remember things longer if you write them down at https://www.lifehack.org/articles/productivity/you-will-remember-information-longer-you-hand-write-notes.html

CHAPTER 7

I have read numerous books as a musician on posture and avoiding injuries and some of the best include Alcantara, Pedro, de. 1997, *Indirect Procedures.* (Oxford University Press, 1997)

Gerald Klickstein, 2009, *The Musicians Way: A guide to practice, performance and wellness,* (Oxford University Press, 2009)

Judith Kleinman and Peter Buckoke, *The Alexander Technique for musicians,* (Bloomsbury, 2013.)

CHAPTER 8

For a deeper insight into myelin see David Coyles, *The Talent code* ((Penguin Random House, 2009) and Dr Molly Gebrian writing on *Music and the brain* available online at https://mollygebrian.com/writing/ (28th October 2021)

CHAPTER 10

Stravinsky quote- https://quotefancy.com/quote/1433240/Igor-*Stravinsky-There-is-music-wherever-there-is-rhythm-as-there-is-life-wherever-there,* 28th October 2021)

CHAPTER 13

To learn more about the research into Mental practice see https://www.frontiersin.org/articles/10.3389/fnhum.2015.00573/full Pascual-Leone, A., et al. (1995). *Modulation of muscle responses evoked by transcranial magnetic stimulation during the acquisition of new fine motor skills.* Journal of Neurophysiology 74(3): 1037-1045.

Elbert, T., et al. (1995). *Increased cortical representation of the fingers on the left hand in string players.* Science 270(5234): 305-307.

CHAPTER 15

There are many good books on overcoming perfectionism and imposter syndrome. One of my personal favourites with phrases that I could quote from all day is David Bayles and Ted Orland's book, *Art and Fear.* (Image Continuum Press 2001).

Richard Ingham's *The Cambridge Companion to the Saxophone,* (Cambridge University Press 1999) is an informative read on the history and development of the instrument. It covers a variety of styles and techniques with contributions from some the world's best performers.

For more exercises to develop awareness in music see. Barry Green's *The Inner Game of Music,* (UK 2015) 54.

Selected Bibliography

Alcantara, Pedro, de, 1997, *Indirect Procedures*. (1997). Oxford University Press, Oxford.

Bayles David, Orland, Ted, 2001, *Art and Fear*. Image Continuum Press.

Boettcher, Michael, Boettcher, Johannes, Mieth, Stefan, Krebs, Thomas, Bergholz, Robert,; Reinshagen, Konrad, *The spaced learning concept significantly improves training for laparoscopic suturing: a pilot randomized controlled study*, Surgical endoscopy volume 32, accessed online October 28, 2021, at pnas.org.

Boettcher, Michael,; Boettcher, Johannes,; Mietzsch, Stefan,; Krebs, Thomas,; Bergholz, Robert,; Reinshagen, Konrad, *Synaptic evidence for the efficacy of spaced learning* accessed online October 28, 2021, at pnas.org.

Buch, E., Claudino, L., Quentin, R., Bönstrup,M., Cohen, L., June 30, 2021, *Consolidation of human skill linked to waking hippocampo - neocortical replay*, volume 35, issue 10, 109193, accessed online October 28, 2021, at cell.com.

Coyles, David, 2009, *The Talent code*, Penguin Random House, London.
Elbert, T., et al. ., 1995, *Increased cortical representation of the fingers on the left hand in string players*. Science 270(5234): 305-307.

Gardner, Ben, D. 2012, *Busting the 21 days habit formation myth*, University College of London accessed online October 2021, UCL blog *https://blogs.ucl.ac.uk/bsh/tag/66-days/*.

Gebrian, Molly, Dr., Music and the Brain accessed online on October 28, 2021 at https://mollygebrian.com/writing/

Gladwell, Maurice, 2008, *Outliers: The Story of Success,* Little, Brown, New York.

Green, Barry, 2015 *The Inner Game of Music,* Pan Macmillan, Basingstoke.

Hyatt, Michael, 2018, *Your Best Year Ever, A 5 step plan for achieving your most important goals*, Baker books, Bath.

Ingham, Richard, 1999, *The Cambridge Companion to the Saxophone*, (Cambridge University Press, Cambridge.

Klickstein, Gerald, *2009, The Musicians Way: A guide to practice, performance and wellness*, Oxford University Press, Oxford.

Kleinman, Judith,; Buckoke, Peter, 2013, *The Alexander Technique for musicians*, Bloomsbury, London.

Matthews, Gail, Dr, 2015, *Study focuses on strategies for achieving goals, resolutions*, Dominican University, California.

Pascual-Leone, A., et al., 1995. *Modulation of muscle responses evoked by transcranial magnetic stimulation during the acquisition of new fine motor skills*. Journal of Neurophysiology 74(3): 1037-1045.

Walker, *Matthew, 2018, Why we Sleep: The New Science of Sleep and Dreams,* Penguin books, e-book edition 111-112

Werners, Kenny, 1996, *Effortless Mastery*, Jamey Aebersold Jazz, New Albany.

Acknowledgements

It's almost impossible to accomplish anything without the love, support and guidance of others- and this book is a true testament to that. First and foremost, I'd like to thank my parents, Lorraine and David Berry; without their encouragement, I would not be where I am today. You were the ones who planted the seed of possibility and passion within me for everything I have accomplished. Thank you for always being there and for the boundless love that you've always surrounded me with. To my partner David Walsh, who I love dearly- It's often said that we take our pain out on those who are closest to us. I know in writing this book, you have also ridden the many waves of hope and possibility, but also those of frustration and fear. Thank you for believing, encouraging and supporting me through the whole process of writing this book. Words cannot express how much I love you, but know it's more than to the moon and back. Thank you to my sister, Susie Burgess, her husband David and my wonderful nephews Jacob and William. You are always there whenever I need help, with no questions asked.

I also want to thank all those who've given me guidance throughout my musical journey so far. There are too many teachers to mention, but a special shout out to Bob Marsh, Richard Ingham and Richard Eastham. Also, a shout out to Stephen Martin, Barbara Tatlock and Dave Jones for their support during my teaching years in education - I couldn't have won all those accolades without you. This brings me on to all the students that I've taught over the past 25 plus years. Thank you - I couldn't be the teacher I am today if you hadn't given me the opportunities, support and, at times, challenges to overcome.

Thank you to my online community for putting your trust in me. A shout out must go to Douglas Park for believing in the Learn Music Together Academy from Day 1. To Sandy Specht for the generous donation to help bring this book to fruition and her continued support. You are a true friend, and I hope one day to meet you in person. Thanks also to Alison Keepax for the image of 'how not to sit while you play the piano', and to all the members for sharing their stories to inspire you the reader. I also would like to thank my accountability partner, Sarah Griffith for all her encouragement and support over recent years. I would not have learnt so many new skills without you. Special thanks to Rita Gornall and Paul Blackburn at Preeta press for all their hard work and guidance in putting this book together. Thank you also to my marvellous editor, Carol Cleary whose attention to detail can be felt on each of these pages.. A huge shout out to Derek Lawton for designing such a thoughtful, creative and beautiful front cover and to James Stretton for introducing us.

Finally I'd like to thank my grandparents, who sadly are no longer with us, but they are always close to my heart. I know you would be so very very proud of this book and everything my family and me have achieved.

Thank you xo

Play with Vitality and Confidence as you Unlock a New Musical You!

"I can already tell a difference within one day a practice."

"It's definitely made me practice in a more structured way and I've made a lot of progress in the last 12 months."

"The whole thing is very, very motivating and very possible."

"LMT is the friendliest group of people, who have a real passion for music. We support and encourage each other."

"Since joining the membership, I do feel more confident, especially when starting a new piece. It's fun to play together and work at getting better."

Learn how to Play Music Better with the Learn Music Together Academy. Helping adults gain new musical heights in their music making.

If you are interested in joining, you can learn more by visiting: https://learnmusictogether.com/membership or open the QR code using the camera on your mobile phone.

About the Author

Fiona is a music examiner for Trinity College London and an International adjudicator. She has a degree in musical performance from Huddersfield university and is a Licentiate member of the Royal Schools of Music, Trinity College London and the London College of Music.

Passionate about helping people fulfil their musical potential, Fiona teaches practice methods that are fun and rewarding through her company Learn Music Together, helping adults attain new heights in their music making and play with confidence.

She has directed numerous prize-winning ensembles and has performed on stages around the world, including the prestigious Montreux Jazz Festival and the World Saxophone Congress.

On her days off you'll find Fiona in the greenhouse, or taking pictures of the wildlife in and around her home on the West Pennine Moors, Lancashire.

learnmusictogether.com

a BIG ask!

Thank You For Reading My Book.

I really appreciate all of your feedback, and I love hearing what you have to say.

I would love your input to make the next version of this book, and my future books even better.

Please leave me a helpful review on Amazon, and let me know what you thought of the book.

By doing so you'll be helping other adult learners like yourself gain the knowledge they need to practice smarter and enjoy playing more music.

Thank you so much!

Fiona

Printed in Great Britain
by Amazon

18118370R00180